LINCOLN CHRISTIAN COLLEGE AND SEMINARY

P9-DFM-100

Many Nations Under God

Ministering to Culture Groups in America

A compilation from persons representing various cultures

New Hope
Birmingham, Alabama

Woman's Missionary Union
P. O. Box 830010
Birmingham, AL 35283-0010
©1997 by Woman's Missionary Union

All rights reserved. First printing 1997
Printed in the United States of America

Dewey Decimal Classification: 259
Subject Headings: CHRISTIAN MINISTRY
ETHNOLOGY
ETHNIC RELATIONS
CROSS CULTURAL STUDIES

Unless otherwise indicated, scripture quotations are from
Contemporary English Version. Copyright © American Bible
Society 1991. Used by permission.
   Scripture quotations indicated by NIV are from the Holy
Bible, New International Version. Copyright © 1973, 1978,
1984 International Bible Society. Used by permission of
Zondervan Bible Publishers.

ISBN: 1-56309-194-1

N973108•0597•5M1

Many Nations Under God

A WORD FROM
THE EDITOR

When a group of contributing authors gathered to collaborate on this book, no one knew exactly what was in store. Each writer had this assignment: *Describe what it is like for a person of your culture to live in the United States of America.*

After opening prayer and a few words of instruction, they began their narratives. For several hours we listened to each account of triumph and trial in this great land of opportunity. We laughed at familiar human foibles and shared the pain of loneliness and mistrust—the offspring of social ignorance and misunderstanding.

As we listened, we recognized a pattern in each story—the sense of aloneness in our worries; the fear that we would be misunderstood or rejected; the desire to be accepted completely for what we are from the heart, no matter how that should differ from the prescribed social norms. We heard the cry, like a persistent echo from each culture, to give the gospel a voice easily understood by those who still cling to their cultural roots as their chief measure of personhood. We soon realized a common confession, that though we each represent a part of the cultural mosaic that is the United States, as Christians we share equally in the spiritual inheritance and love of Christ.

1

We heard each other and we understood that as the colors of the rainbow characterize its beauty, so the variety of God's people is the flourish of the human race. When we see the rainbow, we view it not as a phenomenon of diversity but as a unit complete because of its composition. Likewise, our authors agreed that to be able to see harmony in the diversity among us is an important beginning for ministry among the culture groups in our nation.

Many Nations Under God is a revealing, personal ministry journal. It is a primer for building relationships with restorative intent across the cultures of our land. It acknowledges that though our process for reaching diverse groups does mean effective use of specific knowledge of each group, our mission, our message, and our gospel remain constant. True, not all the answers we will need are contained within, but one stepping-stone leads to another . . . and another . . . and another. It is our prayer that as we take each step, we will draw closer to each fellow servant in this mission of cosmic dimensions.

Ele Clay
West Indian American

INTRODUCTION

Ele Clay

Life in a mix of cultures is doubly difficult, and no mistaking it.[1] My adaptation on Scott Peck's famous opening line aptly describes for me the challenges I faced living within a culture different from the one in which I was born and raised. I suppose I can call myself a West Indian American. (I was born on the island of Trinidad and eventually became the only member of my immediate family to emigrate to the United States.) My premature conclusion that my native English would lift me up and over the cultural adjustments I would find necessary in my new home was the ultimate in naïveté. I suppose one has to live it to understand fully that culture is far more than the language you use to communicate. Some would strongly argue that culture is the fabric of your being.

As we are well aware in this country, the difficulties of coping with a cultural mix also exist in a reverse situation. For it is at best disquieting and at worst xenophobic to find oneself surrounded by images, sounds, smells, and assorted other of the paraphernalia of life that trigger no fond memories of one's home and family. Like the snug fit of the skin wrapped around the vessels-and-bone frame of our physique, the behaviors and social customs of our heritage seem to be as prescribed and immovable. We want them with us like portable barricades, insulating and isolating us. We may live totally unaware that ALL of life is a learning process with the acquisition of culture the greatest quotient of it all.

The difference between this and any other kind of learning is that few of us ever reach a place of comfort with the influences that encroach upon our social selves in new and unfamiliar environments. Somewhere along the way, we fail to receive this helpful tip: *Not all that is different about others is bad and not all that is dear to us is good.* Like the ancients who believed the sun revolved around the earth, we are, in our cultural optics, far more inclined to see ourselves as the center around which all others revolve (or should). The result? The human tendency to draw ourselves into our own understanding and perceive a threat in every unknown. It is common and understandable and it is the psychological extreme outside the circle of cross-cultural interaction and relationship.

What does all this mean in our quest to be the agents of God for good to all the nations?

When the Matthew 28:18–20 passage was spoken, our Lord Jesus was not exclusive in His command to make disciples of all. We cannot deny the wording of His commission to them to reach "all nations." At the time of Christ's ascension Jerusalem was already a cosmopolitan city—a crossroads for the nations of the then-known world. Having witnessed Jesus' intentional ministry to those within and without the fold of Judaism, His disciples knew that His compassion encompassed all of humanity. Indeed, Peter's first sermon and the manifestation of the Holy Spirit at Pentecost were unmistakable confirmation that Christ's words were for literal action. And the Holy Spirit made it so!

Yet, even as the church was finding itself as a common fellowship in its new faith, social fracture lines began to reappear. Within the body of believers, groups began to consolidate around shared concerns, and dissatisfactions arose. The old wounds of separateness that began at Babel (see Gen. 11) resurfaced among believers who failed to recognize the disruptive power of ethnocentric attitudes and behaviors. Like us today, many probably were unaware of their partiality to their own people, insensitive to similar allegiances among those outside their group, and well able to defend the rights they claimed as their own. They had missed the Pentecost revelation, that the *one* gospel, *one* faith, *one* baptism, *one* Lord were manifest for *all.* At Pentecost, the many languages of the Babel dispersion resurged in the many voices of the Spirit calling all to unity in Christ. What at one time separated the prideful human race was sanctified by the Spirit to call us together to worship and witness.

"Make disciples of all nations," the commission Jesus gave to His disciples before leaving the earth, hinged on the authority given to Him by the Father (v. 18). What at first may have appeared to be a manageable assignment soon turned into a life-endangering adventure.

Jesus knew this. He assured His followers that the Holy Spirit would empower them to do His bidding (Acts 1:8). Jesus foresaw the *"adventure*—the bold, exciting, and somewhat dangerous undertaking"[2] in all its dimensions. He understood the ostracism that His followers would suffer for the sake of His message. He knew the inevitable factions that would develop within the ranks of the faithful. He Himself had been accused of partiality to the outcast and dishonorable. He was not unaware of the circles of cultural comfort in which we would hide His truth, and He stood ready to reveal His acceptance of the foreigner with dynamic certainty (see Acts 10–11:18).

And in case we should miss His other provisions, God dramatically called out a strong champion to the Gentiles— Paul. Chosen to carry God's name before the Gentiles and their kings (see Acts 9:15), Paul also became the author of a collection of letters to new churches, a byproduct of his evangelistic and pastoral fervor. These letters of instructions

went to those who were less schooled in the history of
God's dealings with His creation. Throughout the centuries,
the letters became our primary source of church doctrine.
Paul not only declared Christ's "deculturized" gospel, he
stood firm on the fact that God, the Savior and Sovereign of
every nation, tribe, people, and language, holds us account-
able for reaching our generation of cultures, peoples, and
nations with the unifying love of Christ.

But herein lies the paradox. As long as we are comfort-
ably uninformed, we can remain aloof to major scourges in
our society today—communal discord, sometimes fatal up-
heavals caused by hatred, distrust, and apathetic disdain for
those who are different from us. The historic grasping for
more and the struggle for a better life for self and family
that has made some nations great and desecrated others,
still plague us in what we call the most technologically ad-
vanced society of all time.

In our nation, self-proclaimed leader of this age, we
have gathered representative numbers from all the nations
of the earth. Many of these persons, like me, have become
citizens of the United States. We have sworn to uphold the
Constitution that was created over the objections of the un-
recognized nations who possessed the land before the
founding fathers staked their claim. That makes us all part
of one problem and yet part of a great solution. We are part
of the problem because our model of self-assurance tempts
us in one way or another to see ourselves as better than the
other. Yet we are part of the solution, the bridge across the
cultural divide, in that God has given to us, His disciples,
the message and ministry of reconciliation. Together they
represent the witness of eternal salvation and the living testimony of our oneness in Christ.

The nations of the world exist under the sovereignty of
God. To them He has a message we are called to proclaim
in whatever language or cultural context we encounter in
our traverse through life. In His providence, God also has
called our nation to that bold, exciting, and somewhat

dangerous undertaking—ministry to the nations of the world who live, indeed, within its borders.

Why *bold?* It takes a leap of faith outside the security of our own familiar pathways to reach, with concern, into the lives and interests of others. The dilemma of cultural identification is as studied today as any other subject in our time. Groups of people of diverse origin are piquing our interest and intellect as they publicly confront the nuances of this multifaceted issue. They share of themselves to create what common understanding is needed to interrelate and narrow the gap of global relationship. In this book we have just such an entree. Its writers represent several of the nationalities now gathered beneath our flag. Its text gives us confidence to begin a journey into just a few of the cultural life-streams that surround us in our land of many peoples.

Why *exciting?* Because people and their technologies are taking on the challenge of finding ways to breach the linguistic gaps that limit our dialogue in this land where freedom of speech is highly prized. No more can we claim that the fluent grasp of a different language is a critical barrier to ministry. Because we in the United States are such avid consumers, we have spurred a greater access to language skills development than we ourselves realize. This access is both technological and human. For interspersed in the cultural milieu are those whose openness and ability for bilingual dialogue is a gift and a promise of a finer bond. *Many Nations Under God* helps to open a similar curtain of light through those who live and minister within the sometimes murky waters of cross-cultural communication. In Christian love, they speak truths that endure the complexities of discourse.

Why *a dangerous undertaking?* A term so easily descriptive of the challenges that shadow our small, tentative steps across the edges of our cultures. What we perceive to be dangerous can be so in fact equally as much as it can be a recognition of our own limitations. And in our encounters with another culture, our lack of knowledge defines our boundaries. What we cannot do, as we fix our purpose on reaching the nations, is confine ourselves to our cultural boundaries. God has declared the world to be His, and we share our spiritual inheritance with a global fellowship. "That all of them may be one, Father" was the prayer of our Savior. He sealed that pledge with His blood, despising the danger His followers foresaw, so that we may be one.

Many Nations Under God opens for us a tiny window on the kind of vulnerability to which we are called as messengers of a single gospel to a diverse world. The integrity of our witness ebbs and flows on the tide of our genuine love that

   . . . is patient
   . . . is kind
   . . . does not boast
   . . . is not proud
   . . . is not rude
   . . . is not self-seeking
   . . . keeps no record of wrongs
   . . . but rejoices with the truth
   . . . always protects
   . . . always trusts, always hopes, always perseveres
   . . . NEVER FAILS.

No more excellent way is there outside the healing, reconciling grace of Christ. May the spirit of love which binds together the hearts of those who wrote this text strengthen your resolve and stretch the margin of your witness beyond the limits of your cultural horizon.

---

[1]M. Scott Peck, MD, "Life Is Difficult," in *The Road Less Traveled* (New York: Simon and Schuster, 1978), 15.
[2]Thorndike-Barnhart's *World Book Encyclopedia Dictionary*, 1964.

TEXTUAL NOTES

United States of America/America
The United States of America occupies only a portion of the continent of North America, yet often refers to itself as America. In acknowledgement of the fact that other countries on the continent do have a claim to "America" that does not include the US, an attempt has been made in this text to limit the use of *America* as referring solely to the United States.

Cultural Identifications
One of the key issues in the discussion of cultural recognition and acceptance is the ability to identify one's uniqueness as a contribution to the whole. Because of the growing openness to cultural diversity in our nation and the many forums now available for expressing one's cultural heritage, it has become popular and acceptable for ethnic groups to identify both their roots and their allegiance to the United States.

The term *hyphenated American* is used by some to disparage attempts to display the very birthrights of which some ethnic groups are proud. Thankfully, it is honored more often as a banner of connectivity—with the source from which one is irreversibly connected by natural birth and the spirit of this nation in which we now invest our lives, our possessions, and our vision.

9

RICHES BEYOND THE BARRIER:
Biblical Models for Cross-cultural Relationships

Gary Furr

During our seminary days, my wife was a head resident at a women's dorm at Campbell University. As "dorm mother" she took care of nearly 100 young women. Many were from the South, but many came from other regions of the United States. We also had students from other lands.

One day at the dorm, we heard two sisters from the Middle East crying loudly in the television room. My wife went to see what was wrong with them. When they calmed down, they told her that their father had placed a certain amount of money in their joint account to last them for the entire school year. It was now only November, one sister sobbed, and they were afraid that their money would not last until May.

My wife returned to tell me about their plight and we discussed what we might do. After all, we were a struggling seminary family! We got the only $20 bill we had and she rolled it up to take to them. She came back laughing. "What's so funny?" I inquired.

"Well," she said, "They were upset because their father had placed $100,000 in their account and they have already spent $60,000. They are afraid that they can't make it until May on only $40,000 for both of them!" She had brought back the $20 bill!

How often we are surprised by the little we know about others. We are caught with the assumption that other cultures are deficient or defective. We may harbor many stereotypes toward them. What an irony it is! The less contact we have with others, the more likely we are to mistrust them, dislike them, or even hate them.

Thank God that Christianity in the New Testament breaks down these inward barriers. The Christian gospel is an invitation for us to trust God and allow our minds and hearts to be enlarged by the world around us. But putting it into practice is quite a challenge!

What are the qualities required to cross the barriers that divide us from others? These four Bible stories can help us find ways to be more open in Christ to others not simply for the sake of the Christian gospel but also so we might discover, beyond our fears and misunderstanding, the wonderful richness of the world that God loves so deeply.

Learning to See the Person
Ruth

Ruth was a Moabite. The Moabites were from what is now the nation of Jordan. The Moabites worshiped their own tribal god, Chemosh. They were despised enemies of Israel during much of the Old Testament period. However, at the time of the Book of Ruth, Israel and Moab lived in peace.

Ruth was the daughter-in-law of Naomi, a Hebrew woman. Naomi and her husband, Elimelech, had moved to Moab during a famine. The time came when Naomi's husband died. Her sons both married young women from Moab. Naomi's sons also died, and the ties that bound Naomi and her two daughters-in-law dissolved. They were free to go, and the Bible reports that one, Orpah, did return to her home (Ruth 1:8–15), though she loved Naomi.

At this point, Ruth declares her fidelity to her mother-in-law in the passage that has become so familiar as part of our wedding ceremonies:

"Please don't tell me to leave you and return home! I will go where you go, I will live where you live; your people will be my people, your God will be my God" (Ruth 1:16–17).

What is startling is that Ruth is not affirming a biological or marital commitment. She is declaring love and loyalty where none is required! When Naomi saw Ruth's determination, she did not send her away. All this may have been part of the curiosity they stirred when they came to Bethlehem, where Naomi's family still lived (Ruth 1:19).

Obviously from the rest of the story, Ruth and Naomi have learned to love and appreciate each other. They have not only common love for their husbands' family but also admiration and respect for one another. Their ingenuity and cleverness enable them to survive and thrive in a man's world. But we also see how important their love and fellowship are in sustaining them.

Naomi won the love and respect of her daughters-in-law in ways that transcended what was required. Ruth had qualities of love and loyalty that exceeded the minimum. They glimpsed into one another's hearts. It is here that we must begin if we are to build relationships across cultural lines.

We must be intentional about loving others. If we are to reach those who are different from us, it will be done through relationships.

The New Testament describes a church that is spirit filled. One of the signs of that filling is a willingness to cross lines and meet people who are out of our usual circles. This is always possible but not always comfortable to do. The purpose of outreach is not market share, not accommodation to the culture, not success, not growth. It is conversion, that mysterious, spiritual process by which a person who is in a Moab of one sort or another comes into contact with a loving heart and through that heart begins to consider that this God may indeed be real. By faith they reach out and find themselves willing to leave their culture behind, not in exchange for another culture so much as for the true and living God.

R. A. Torrey told the story of a young woman in England who always wore a golden locket and would not allow anyone to look into it. Everyone thought surely that this contained a picture of her beloved or some romantically significant thing. She died at an early age, and after her death, the locket was opened. Inside was simply a slip of paper that had these words of Scripture written on them: "Whom having not seen, I love."

Isn't this where we must begin? We must be willing, by faith, to love the unknown, the other. After all, we cannot love Jesus unless our hearts leap across the centuries to the pages of Scripture, written in a different language and culture, to love a Man Who loved us first. Such enlargement of the heart makes it possible for us to reach across the cultural barriers of today as well.

The "leaving behind" is not one-sided, however. Naomi also had to open herself to those who were different. To reach out to others is a challenge. Is there room in our hearts to love strangers like Naomi loved these two foreign young women? If we would be evangelistic, we would say, "Of course." And our deeds would match our words.

Dealing with Negative Attitudes
Jonah

Most popular discussion about the Book of Jonah focuses on the "whale." This is unfortunate. "Great fish" is the actual translation of the Hebrew, so it is not clear whether it was a whale or some other great fish that swallowed Jonah. I purposely describe this "fish focus" as unfortunate. The debate over whether this incident actually happened or not (important as that is) misses the whole point of the story!

The Book of Jonah is about a stubborn prophet whose heart is resistant to God. God calls Jonah to go to Nineveh and preach that the people of Nineveh must repent, for judgment is at hand. Jonah refuses and runs away. He hops aboard a ship bound for Tarshish, as far from Nineveh as the people of that time knew about.

God sends a storm upon them. They discover that Jonah is the cause and that he is running from God. Jonah begs them to throw him overboard. At first they refuse. But finally, seeing no other course, they relent and toss him into the deep, where he is swallowed by a great fish and resides within it for three days. While Jonah is in the fish's belly, God deals with his heart. Jonah calls out to God. God hears him and causes the fish to vomit Jonah out upon the dry land.

The Book of Jonah emphasizes a sovereign God. It also stresses that we resist God's will in our lives to our own disadvantage. But the Book of Jonah is preeminently a story that points out how wrong our narrow exclusion of others can be.

Jonah goes to Nineveh and preaches. Nineveh was the capital of the Assyrian empire, the hated superpower that oppressed Israel in Jonah's time. When the people repent, God decides in His merciful love to spare them instead of sending the judgment He originally promised. Jonah's reaction is all too human! He becomes angry.

Jonah sits on a hill to wait and see if perhaps God might destroy the city anyway. God then causes a plant to grow up and shade Jonah's head from the heat. Jonah is so happy that the plant has come! Then God sends a worm to destroy the plant. Jonah becomes furious about the plant's death.

God uses the occasion to teach Jonah a lesson. If he can become so angry about one plant's death, why should God not care about the deaths of thousands of people in Nineveh?

This lesson is not lost on us either! We harbor many harsh attitudes toward others that can cause us to run away from opportunities to know those who may be different from us. When those attitudes are revealed by the light of God, we see them for what they are—petty, self-centered, immature, or even wicked. Who are we, indeed, to tell the God of the universe whom He may love, whom He may redeem, or whom we should love?

Unfortunately, these attitudes are hidden deep within. We must plunge into the deep, like Jonah's descent into the sea, to uncover them. Our culture sometimes confirms them. After I got to know some Arab friends, I began to recognize how many vicious portrayals of Arab people often occur in US media. I have noticed many other such portrayals that confirm or play up to popular stereotypes.

Part of this originates in the human heart. We do not wish to face painful truth. It is far easier to run from it. We run in many ways, but one of the most familiar ways is to attribute our own deepest failings onto someone else.

I once saw a cartoon in which a woman said of another woman sitting in an ice cream parlor, "That woman must have an eating problem. I come in here nearly every day and she is always here, buying ice cream." We sometimes see in others that which we most despise in ourselves . . . or that which we fear.

We must be careful of where our anger goes, of what we listen to, what we are willing to believe. When we say, "Those people . . . " we are not far from the sin of Jonah. God loves His entire creation.

To build friendships across cultural lines, we must be willing to face long-held attitudes. Some of these attitudes are part of our culture. Some are misunderstandings that have come from unfortunate contacts we have had or bad relationships with someone from another group of people. Some are simply based on irrational ideas that we have held without knowing their source.

Because these beliefs can be so deep, it takes "surgery of the soul" to overcome them. Often it takes a spiritual crisis to force us to see these truths. We might wish that we did not have to make such a journey. Yet, for many of us, there is no other way. We must face the truth that such attitudes contradict the purposes of the great God of heaven and earth.

Are we willing, like Jonah, to face that and turn? If so, we can learn anew of the love of God for ourselves as well.

Releasing the Past
Jesus and the Woman at the Well
As we look into our hearts, we may discover that, just as

Jonah did, we harbor resentments, misunderstandings, or
culturally biased attitudes. Once we have faced the truth
that our negative attitudes toward others do not please God,
we still must do something about it! Jesus shows us the
way. In the wonderful story of the woman at the well, we
see Jesus' example of crossing the boundaries of misunderstanding.

When Jesus comes to the well and asks for water, the
woman says in John 4:9, "'How can you ask me for a drink
of water when Jews and Samaritans won't have anything to
do with each other?'"

That single statement in John 4:9 contains centuries of
bitter history. This may be hard for us to see because we
often focus more on the personal situation of the woman.
We marvel at the power of God's love to reach a woman
who had had five husbands and now was living with someone who was not her husband! This passage has been
meaningful for us to talk about evangelism and encouragement for those whose lives are disasters. But this story is
also about Jews and Samaritans.

When the Jews returned from exile in the Persian period, 538–332 B.C., this provoked envy on the part of
Judah's neighbors, the Samaritans. After 722 B.C., Israelites
left in the north had intermingled with foreign settlers (see 2
Kings 17). The Samaritans were therefore not recognized as
true Israelites.

At first Samaritans continued to worship in Jerusalem,
but eventually they sought their own place of worship. This
explains their common Scripture but different places of worship. During the rule of Alexander the Great, the Samaritans
received permission to build a temple on Mount Gerizim.

The hatred between the groups only increased when, in
128 B.C., the Jews under John Hyrcanus destroyed the
Samaritan temple. Though it was not rebuilt, they cling to
the place as holy even today. *Samaritan* was a Jewish term
of abuse. We see in John 8:48 that it is applied to Jesus as
an ethnic slur.

In His contact with the woman of Samaria, Jesus does two remarkable things. First, he intentionally enters into relationship with the woman and with the Samaritan people. We miss the cross-cultural significance of Jesus' trip through Samaria. John tells us, "He had to pass through Samaria." Some of His contemporaries might have responded, "I would travel out of my way to avoid going there!" Jesus faces the difficulties between His own people and these alienated ones.

Second, Jesus probes the misunderstandings that exist between the Samaritans and the Jews. As He usually does, Jesus reveals to the woman the limitations of their cultural concepts and replaces them with the higher calling of the kingdom of God. "But a time is coming, and it is already here! Even now the true worshipers are being led by the Spirit to worship the Father according to the truth. These are the ones the Father is seeking to worship him" (John 4:23). *Until our priorities are right, we will still be slaves to the limited views of our own group.* God is greater than all the local claims of human groups.

Now we can see the parable of the Good Samaritan (Luke 10:30 37) and the Samaritan leper (Luke 17:11–19) in a different light. Jesus calls His hearers' ancient assumptions into radical question.

The early Christian church also made this leap to receive the Samaritans (Acts 8:4–25). Jesus was transforming the past when he "had to go to Samaria." He called into question six centuries of competition and resentment. He destroyed the justifications for their separation and declared that in Him a new possibility for fellowship existed.

We often harbor secret misconceptions of others and are rarely honest or trusting enough with one another to lay them on the table and see them for what they are. When we do, however, Christ can transform them, enable us to forgive and let go, so that we might take up life and fellowship with others in a new way!

Listening to the Spirit
Philip and the Ethiopian

Church growth advocates tell us, "Location is everything."
Acts 8 reveals that Philip hears a voice that says, "Go to the
desert." Today's leader would have argued with the angel,
"Hey! You'll never reach people here. There's only one guy
in a chariot." And, truth was, he was a eunuch slave of the
Ethiopian queen. He was a foreigner, an African who was
unclean in the eyes of the law, incapable even of biological
reproduction.

But go, Philip was told, and he went. Then again, the
angel said, "Go join him in the chariot." What a strange circumstance! Yet early church tradition has it that this man
evangelized Ethiopia and that the fruit of that one visit still
lives there today. How could Philip know beforehand that
this desert trip could bear such fruit?

Often it is in the most unlikely places that good erupts.
No guide can lead us there. We just go. Which is why the
real growth of the church will happen not by techniques
and programs but by yielding our hearts before the Holy
Spirit.

It may seem a waste of time to go after the unlikely
people, those who don't fit our congregational profile or
those who are different from us. The question for Christians
is about what God's Spirit is saying to us. It is not simply a
matter of affirming that God can break down barriers. The
Book of Acts is saying that breaking down barriers IS the
work of the Spirit.

If we want Jesus to come into our hearts, we must open
them. Once we open them for Jesus, however, we also
open them for others. We cannot have it both ways. We
cannot have Jesus and also close our hearts to others. *To
step across the differences means we must listen to and obey
God's Spirit.*

THE ORIGINAL AMERICANS

Emerson Falls

I am from Phoenix, Arizona. I am a member of the Sauk/Sac and Fox Nation. When I was 16 years old, I became a Christian. This event took place during a period in my life when I was trying to fit in a lot. I became a Christian in an Anglo church where I found a certain amount of acceptance, but I did hear comments. During my senior year, I dated a girl whose father was a deacon in the church I attended. When the time came for our senior prom, I naturally invited her to go with me. She accepted. A couple of days later she told me couldn't go. When I asked why, she said her father didn't want her to go with me. He had told her that somewhere in the Bible it was written that it was wrong to mix blood. Therefore she concluded that she could not go, simply because of who I was. I remember that painful memory of really hurting because somehow I wanted to be white and I couldn't be. I was constantly reminded that I could not be what I was not. It's been bad to be Indian, but we can't be other than what we are.

I soon came to the place, in my college years I guess, where I became angry. I became very angry with a lot of things. I tried to be militant even though I was not very much inclined in that direction. I had a lot of bitterness. I had a lot of hate in my life. I confess, I hated white people because I felt that they were the cause of the situation in which we lived. But I didn't know what to do. No reservations existed in which I could find the quality of life I wanted to have. I belonged nowhere. I didn't want to be part of the White society, but there wasn't anything attractive in Indian culture that I wanted. That has been the struggle, and continues to a certain extent to be a struggle. I struggled for identity, for healthy self-esteem, always feeling somehow that I was second-class in a lot of ways.

When I became very bitter, I did a lot of things that were self-destructive. Then I rediscovered my faith in Jesus Christ and He began to change my life. I began to find something that I could never find in my culture or in the dominant culture—Someone Who accepted me as I am. I can't tell you how important that is to me. I began to gain a certain amount of self-acceptance. My life began to change. I began to realize that I was an angry person, that anger was self-destructive, and that I was self-destructing as a human being. I did not want to do that.

After I was married, I wanted to raise my kids in a different kind of society. So I began to discover who we, as Native Americans, are as a people. I began to discover some things about our culture that are very beautiful. I developed a sense of pride. One of the things I do today is struggle to live in two cultures. But I identify with my Sauk and Fox culture, my Native American culture, by choice! Because that's who I am and I'm proud of who I am for the first time. I am not ashamed of my people.

I dress the dominant culture, I speak English. In fact, I don't speak the native language well at all because that's one of the things that has been taken from me. But what I want you to know is, I think Native American.

My children will probably marry Anglo, Hispanic, Korean, African American, and that's fine. I accept that. But I'm like you. I want my children to marry a Native American, and if they want to, that's fine. I'm more concerned that they will marry someone who will love them, that they will love.

The Struggle with Identity

Indians, American Indians, Native Americans, terms which
are really misnomers, but they are the words people generally
use to refer to my people. Any one of these words can be a
convenient handle, but none is the way we identify ourselves.

On one occasion, some of our elders were listening to a
group explain to them why people call us *Indians*. One of
the younger ones who was educated tried to explain that
this man, Columbus, had been sailing west, looking for the
Indies. When he came to this continent he assumed he had
found the Indies. The people that he saw he called *Indians*.
One of our elders responded, "Well, I am sure glad he
wasn't looking for Turkey!"

Among ourselves, we don't identify ourselves as *Indians*
or *Native Americans*. Here's why. As a member of the Sauk
and Fox Nation, my culture is different from the Hopa or
the Navajo. As a Sauk and Fox working among the Navajo,
the Hopa, the Apache, in Arizona, I was like a foreign missionary. I had to learn their culture.

It is very important to us that people realize that when
they think about "Native Americans" they must understand
that there is no such person as a *Native American Indian*.
The original people of this continent are more than 500 different tribes and most people have never heard of mine.
When I say Sauk and Fox, people say, "What?! Can you
spell that for me?"

So I have to back up and explain. The easiest way is to
introduce the curious to a little history. I ask two questions:

Number one: Have you ever heard of Jim Thorpe, the
great Olympic athlete? He was Sauk and Fox.

Number two: Have you heard of the great Indian chief
who fought for the British in the War of 1812? He also led
some of the tribe in what is called the Black Hawk War of
1832. Chief Black Hawk was Sauk and Fox.

In our country, it is popular to talk about Cherokees.
When I talk to people who say they are part Cherokee, I always say that the Cherokees must be the biggest tribe in the

world! I rarely hear people admit to having "this much Sauk
and Fox in me." Yet that's who I am.

In a way, this explains what it means to be "Native
American" in the United States today. One of my struggles,
and one I think I share with my people, is the struggle with
an identity, trying to identify who we are.

No Place for Us

When I was a young person, just a little boy in the early
1950s, I was walking in downtown Ardmore, Oklahoma, a
little town in southern Oklahoma. My cousin and I were
thirsty. We went into a department store on the edge of
town, a sort of high-class department store in those days, to
get a drink of water. Those were the days of the segregated
water fountains. We went over to the fountain which had
signs that read White and Colored. My cousin and I looked
at each other and laughed. We went around thirsty all day
because we were neither white nor colored. To our innocent
minds there was no place for us . . . the irony of identity.

Because we "Native Americans" are a small minority, we
have very little visibility. What people know about us they
learn from books and movies that portray a romanticized
version of who we are. We struggle with that.

Part of the reason for the struggle for identity is the
Europeans' historical attempts to Anglicize us. That has always been the history of our people. Understand that the
Christian church, the federal government, and the missionaries had the idea that they were doing us a favor by "civiliz-
ing" us. And so the young ones (even in my generation)
were not allowed to speak their language in the boarding
schools. Their hair was cut. They were not allowed to wear
their traditional dress. Basically each succeeding generation
taught their children the same thing. I remember my father
telling me that if I was going to make it in this world, I
would have to learn the "white man's ways." Therefore, as a
young boy, I essentially wanted to be white. That was the
society in which I wanted to live.

Now we are not sure who we are. We struggle with
what it means to be an Indian. If you go to the reservations
in Arizona today, in particular, the San Carla Apache
Reservation, you will become aware of the prevalence of
gangs. But if you observe carefully, you'll see that the
Indians that belong to the gangs adopt the culture of the
Hispanic gangs of Los Angeles. They dress like Hispanics
and adopt the Hispanic culture because they don't know
who they are. They adopt that culture in order to identify.
And so the struggle continues.

To Be What We Cannot Be

We cannot be white. I discovered that a long time ago. Part
of this struggle began when I was young. I developed a
negative image of Indians because of the stereotypes that
were commonplace at that time. Western movies of the
1950s were almost at the end of their heyday, but they were
still very significant image builders. I grew up watching
these western movies. Now that I am more conscious of the
realities of identity, watching cowboy and Indian movies is
kind of tough for me. In these movies, Indians were de-
picted as savages and they were always defeated. As a
child, every week I spent 25 or 50 cents to get in to see a
good western. There they were, the larger-than-life screen
images of John Wayne, Gabby Hayes, Maureen O'Hara, always left behind in the wagon train with about half of the
Sioux Nation or half the Cheyenne Nation attacking them.
Yet the Indians always lost the fight!!

When I became a teenager, I would often hear some
well-meaning person wanting to joke, teasing me about
"fire water." "Keep him away from the fire water," they
would say. I would smile on the outside but I was hurting
on the inside as I listened to those comments. To a young
boy, all of this added up. I confess to the fact that there
was a time in my life when I really didn't want to be
Sauk and Fox. I wanted to be white because "that's where
it was at."

I can remember buying a skin lotion that was supposed to lighten the skin at a neighborhood drugstore. I took it to the bathroom, rubbed it on myself and scrubbed my skin with a washcloth. I thought somehow I could wipe my skin and be something that I wasn't. But I was constantly reminded that this was impossible. I would get into fights after school just because somebody wanted to "fight an Indian." No thanks to the character Geronimo and other "tough" Indians in the movies that provoked the idea that beating up a real life Geronimo made a guy macho. I could not escape it. Finally, I came to the point where I got tired of being beaten up, so I decided to fight. I learned to fight, but not because that's my nature. It was a matter of survival. Fighting was one way to survive.

Another incident that vividly reminded me of the futility of changing my skin took place when I was in high school. I was one of two Indians in my public high school. Interestingly enough, we never talked to each other. I suppose the reason was that he probably felt as I did. We didn't want to be seen together, so I didn't know him very well. You would have thought we would have been attracted to each other, but the opposite was true because we were trying to blend into this high school. We wanted to be a part of the majority.

But a change began in the 1960s, the era of the Civil Rights movement and other similar events. As the events unfolded, people began to feel pride in who they were. Indians were a part of this awakening.

Dream versus Reality

I heard people talk about how Indians had it made because the federal government took care of them. As I began to examine the existing situation, I looked at the reservation system and discovered that Indians did not ask to be put on reservations. They were forcefully moved to reservations, and a reservation is not a good place on which to live. You cannot maintain a life on the reservation. The fact that

Indians were reduced to receiving handouts was involuntary. Their choice was to receive handouts or basically starve to death because the land they were put on to farm could not be farmed. The Apaches, for example, were put on the desert regions of Arizona, where there was little water.

The widespread belief that it was a good thing to send our children where they could get a good education— where they could "learn to be white"—resulted in the fact that most of our people grew up in boarding schools. So all our parenting skills were disrupted because a whole generation was raised in federal and Christian boarding schools.

Today, our life expectancy is the lowest of any group in the United States. It varies between approximately 48 to 52 years depending on whose analysis you read. This is believable because we still succumb to such diseases as tuberculosis, a killer among us. Almost 90 percent of Native Americans suffer from diabetes. Suicide is another enemy. We die young. All these and hopelessness help to bring down our life expectancy.

Conflicts with Concepts

I discovered also that the differences in our cultural concepts create conflicts. For instance, ours is an extended family. The father in this extended family would be the older son. He would have the authority. He would be the one to whom we would listen.

Other societies may not place the same importance on the extended family as they do on the immediate family circle. In our culture, aunts and uncles do not carry such designations. For instance, when my uncle died, my wife had difficulty getting time off from work. Her boss said, "It's just your husband's uncle." Yet to us, that is not who he was. He was my father. It is just a different way of looking at the world—a different worldview.

Culturally, we are very person-oriented as opposed to what we describe as the property-oriented culture of the

Anglos. This has been another strong, historical stumbling block between us. When Europeans came in and began to divide the land and draw boundaries, draw property lines, began to have ownership, it was a foreign concept to us. Private ownership was important in the dominant society. But the significance of persons is where we tend to excel.

In the Anglo culture, unless you invited me in, I could not go to your house, enter and help myself to a sandwich because I would be violating your property. In Native American culture, the same goes for respect of personhood. You don't violate another's person. That's why we are not great with handshakes. That's very uncomfortable for us. We are being accommodating to others when we shake hands.

Looking someone in the eye and having a one-on-one conversation is another point of difficulty you'll find with a lot of Native Americans. Until we share a certain amount of familiarity between us, we consider it a violation of your personhood to look you in the eye.

Giving. In our society, our culture, you are honored when you are allowed a chance to give. In the Anglo culture, on birthdays you receive presents. To us, that's backwards. It is the honored person who has the opportunity to give. So on birthdays the family would have a big ceremony. They would buy presents and invite people. To honor me they would give presents to different people. It's different, but it is the ideal—the ideal of emphasizing giving, rather than taking . . . giving back to others.

A visiting evangelist and I went to visit a man who was in the hospital. The preacher was Anglo and we went to visit an Indian fellow. The gentleman was in his hospital bed when we arrived. He turned and reached into his desk drawer where he had only three dollars. He took out a dollar and gave it to me to give to the preacher. The preacher said, "Oh, no, no. Here, you keep it." I took the dollar and put it in my pocket and walked out.

The evangelist confronted me about it. He said, "Man, he only had three dollars." I walked away without explaining that I had ministered to the man when I took that dollar and put it in my pocket. I honored the man by allowing him to give. To me, that is Christian.

When I could see such things in my culture, all of a sudden I discovered, "You know, our culture's not so bad!

An Ancient Culture

Native American culture is at least 10,000 years old. History books say this country was settled from the east to the west. Not so. It was first settled from Alaska, from the northwest to the southeast, from west to east. The second migration was the other way. We've had 10,000 years of immersion in our cultural values and 500 years of Western culture. Those 500 years of Western culture have not erased the influence of our culture, the way we think, or the way we view the world. And so we struggle because we want to be who we are. We're proud of who we are. We don't fit in the dominant society. We accommodate the dominant society, but we want to be "Indian."

Death by Assimilation

One of the tough parts about being a Native American in the United States today is watching the death of my people. As our people become assimilated, not always by choice, but as they become assimilated through the natural process of life in this country, very few of us speak the heart language anymore. The number of full-blooded tribal people is diminishing rapidly. The people who know our traditions are passing away. Within the next two or three generations, there may not be a so-called Native American culture.

What began 500 years ago will find its culmination, probably by the year 2050. Think of it this way: For the Africans there is an Africa; for the Cubans there is a Cuba; for the Koreans there is a Korea; there is no other place for us. This is it. And when we are gone from this land, our culture is gone forever.

For years there will be people who will identify with
Native Americans . . . there will always be people who are
"part Cherokee." But as a culture and as a people, very few
are left. The pool from which to draw is so small. So if you
want to see Native American culture, you need to go to the
reservations now because it will not be here much longer.

Reaching the Native American

Jimmy Anderson

I am of the Creek Tribe and sometimes I am called Jimmy
the Creek! My life has been a wonderful adventure. Looking
back, I see how God worked in my life and how He has
led me to my present place of service—national director for
Native American Baptist ministries for the Southern Baptist
Home Mission Board (now North American Mission Board)
since 1995.

Growing up in the late 1930s and early 1940s, I began
to get an idea of what society thought of American Indians
when I would go to the old Dixie Theater in Holdenville,
Oklahoma. On Saturday afternoons, I, too, watched cowboy
heroes such as Gene Autry, Roy Rogers, and Hopalong
Cassidy. I observed that the bad guys in practically all those
movies were the ones coming over the hills on horseback,
all painted up, yelling, shooting arrows, surrounding a
wagon train, and giving poor helpless settlers burr haircuts!!
How dare those "savages" do that!!

So my earliest recollections of who I am as an Indian
were not very encouraging. You can imagine that my self-esteem was not very high. Society may have thought I was
nothing, but how I rejoiced when I heard my pastor and the
missionary say that God knew me and in His eyes I am
somebody! He created me and sent His Son to die for me!

During a time when my mother was quite ill in an
Indian hospital with the possibility of dying, her concern
was for her three children. She prayed, asking God to spare
her life long enough for us to be grown and on our own.
She promised Him that in return she would no longer take
us to the Creek green corn dances or the stomp dances.
She pledged to take us to the Many Springs Indian Baptist
Church and raise us for Jesus. God heard our mother's
prayer. She got well and we never went back to the Creek
ceremonials, but began attending Many Springs Church. My
mother was faithful to her word. At her death at the age of
78, she was still serving the Lord and was the treasurer of
the church. I thank God for a godly mother who throughout her life, sacrificially and with much prayer, guided us to
live our lives for the Lord.

After I had become a missionary, my mother told me
that she had prayed that one day, one of her two sons
would be a preacher. She began praying about the time I
was still running around the church grounds in "buckskin
pampers," my mother said. She had prayed the preacher
would be me, and she lived long enough to see God answer that prayer. Then I understood how I got through the
turbulent, searching years of my youth. It was because of
my mother's prayers. Life was not easy for her and when
we three children caused her heartache, she wept, prayed,
and urged us to live for the Lord. To me she was beautiful.

In a storefront Indian Baptist church in Oklahoma City,
God began to shape the direction of my life. I fasted three
days because I wanted to know if He was truly calling me
to preach. I was still in college when I surrendered my life
into His service. I prayed that God would let me preach to
as many of my people as possible. Forty years later, He is
still allowing me to do just that!

Following the suggestion of our Creek missionary, B.
Frank Belvin, I began to set my eyes on seminary. Some of
the Indian women contacted other women's missions
groups in the city and they collected offerings to keep me

in school. I owe a debt to these women's groups for the
part they played in my spiritual journey. It was a journey
that led me and my wife, Cowena, into 31 years of service
as missionaries to our Indian people.

Creating a New Past

Ministry to the original Americans is in one of the most
challenging, yet inspiring, periods of missions history. Some
exciting things have happened in the past 15 years as we
have witnessed Native American churches and leaders take
the initiative to reach out in a scope never seen before. This
has resulted in some good gains and positive directions that
are encouraging.

For many years, individuals or church groups have been
sending out Indian missions teams in local areas or across
the country. But 21 years ago, a more concentrated effort at
evangelism took root as a national missions program sending out teams to help begin new Indian ministries or to
help strengthen existing works. You can learn from the re-
port on these works what has worked and continues to
work in developing ministries to Native Americans.

Encouraging Our Youth

In 1982, due to the concern of two Indian women, the
National Indian Baptist Youth Conference was initiated to
reach and encourage our college youth. That conference is
still going strong and reaching upwards of 1,000 in attendance. It is also responsible for sending out student summer
missionaries.

Affirming our Leadership

In 1985, a National Native American Southern Baptist
Fellowship was organized at the Southern Baptist
Convention in Dallas, Texas. The overarching purpose was
to help unify our efforts, set goals and directions, and cooperate with Southern Baptist agencies to reach and develop
ministries among American Indians.

Now, a monthly National First Sunday PrayerTime is being initiated in all Southern Baptist Indian congregations. It focuses on specific areas and needs from Canada, Alaska, and the Lower 48 states, with churches praying specifically for crisis needs in Indian ministries. If Indian missions is to see even greater growth and spiritual victories in the years ahead, then every effort we make must be undergirded by prayer.

Committed Leadership—The Key for Ministry

On the Reservation

Our missionaries and pastors are in the midst of a flurry of activity on the reservations. Churches are sending out Indian missions teams all across the country. Some teams lead Vacation Bible School (VBS), some assist in building projects, and some do survey work.

Other workers such as Andrew Begaye, Navajo missionary, help to develop and train native leaders. Beginning new work often is a result of outreach evangelism and ministering in camp meetings as well as the involvement of both native and other missions teams.

Allen Elston served about 35 years in Oregon on the Warm Springs Reservation. He came to realize quickly that the traditional way of reaching Indian people wasn't working. So he did relational evangelism, which meant going on wild horse roundups, branding cattle, and so forth, to build relationships where he could spread the gospel, particularly among the men. Nineteen years went by before the first Indian man was won to the Lord, but now the church there is growing with strong, committed Indian leadership.

J. B. Fish, Creek pastor to the Seminoles in Florida, involves the elders on visitation. Even those who have to use their canes for mobility are urged to take part. Since they cannot get out of the cars to visit the homes with the younger members, the elders ask Fish why they are included. He tells them that everyone is needed. While the younger members visit, the elders remain in the car and

pray for those in the house and for those who are witnessing. This is a creative way for a pastor to utilize older and
younger members together in reaching people for the Lord
and at the same time bridge the generation gap.

Another missionary, John Bailey, on the Zuni
Reservation, faced the complexing problem of how to minister to a tribe in which clans did not get along together.
"How can you get them together in a worship service?" His
answer—"You don't!" The solution was to have several worship services during the week, by clans. Overall, he reached
more of the people this way than he would have if he had
struggled to bring them together in one meeting. Often, on
a reservation, one has to be flexible and innovative.

Indian pastors and missionaries such as Wilbert
Robertson, North Dakota, and Steve Osage, South Dakota,
can always make use of donated clothing and other vital
necessities to help needy families. Churches and women's
organizations have provided specific assistance with clothing and church supplies. Often serving in places that are
isolated from other Baptist Indian leaders, these faithful ser-
vants struggle against almost overwhelming odds.
Partnership ministries with men such as these assure sup-
portive prayers and supplies for crisis needs.

One Anglo man, Kurt Schafli, working with our Baptist
people, has a burden for reaching the Native American. He
has written a booklet entitled, "Indian Symbols Tell the
Gospel." He takes it onto sacred sun dance grounds and
uses it to show the traditional ceremonial leaders how their
own symbols point to Christ. He relates that most often, he
has been listened to respectfully. While not too many have
openly accepted Christ through this witness, they have no
argument against what they are shown. This man directed
his life to live near the people and to minister to them on a
daily basis. His life and actions demonstrate his Christian
concern for the spiritual welfare of the Indian people.

Other ethnic groups provide a dynamic mix to evangelism on the reservations. Chinese and Korean congregations

have offered their services. One Chinese church in Phoenix helped staff a VBS on the Apache Reservation in Arizona and recorded the largest VBS of any Baptist congregation in the state. That VBS had over 600 in attendance! Korean churches have supported new Indian ministries and have sent youth music teams to Indian youth conferences. Many are continuing to seek ways in which to help. This is one of the most positive missions efforts we are seeing in these days—the networking of ethnic groups to reach various peoples with the gospel of Jesus Christ!

In Metropolitan Areas
Approximately 73 percent of Native Americans live in metropolitan areas. Most of the big cities have a large Indian population that needs to be reached for the Lord. Churches such as Oklahoma City Baptist and Tulsa Indian Baptist use a traditional evangelistic method of an annual citywide Indian crusade.

George Smith, an Oklahoma Creek, spent most of his life ministering to the drug-addicted and alcoholic Indians in the huge city of San Francisco. Smith served until his own death. His legacy—a life of sacrificial giving and love to those imprisoned by sin.

Victor Kaneubbe, Choctaw, now retired but still active, helped First Indian Baptist Church in Phoenix, Arizona, to reach out to the problem drinker. He taught and nurtured young Indian Christians to become vital, active, giving church members. Through his teaching on tithing the church has become financially stable. Young leaders started other ministries. Emerson Falls, Sauk and Fox, followed Kaneubbe as pastor. Under his leadership, the church continued its strong growth. Falls is presently director of a Golden Gate Baptist Theological Seminary satellite center in Denver, Colorado. This is evidence of the high capabilities of many of our Indian leaders.

The First Baptist Church of Tyler, Texas, showed an interest in reaching Indian people in their area. Through the efforts of Dale Seigler, catalytic Indian missionary of Texas, and Oklahoma Indian Baptists, a team of two Indian pastors went to Tyler and did a survey of the city. They contacted Indian families, which resulted in a rally that drew more than 100 people. A follow-up to this rally may determine the start of a new Native American ministry. This illustrates how a caring, local church, along with state leaders and Indian teams, can cooperate together to begin new works.

Glorieta Baptist Church, Oklahoma City, under the leadership of Ledtkev McIntosh, Creek, is reaching all age ranges (many members are young married couples). This vibrant, growing church is training strong leaders who understand the nature of the church. Two satellite ministries were started in order to reach Indian families in neighboring communities. Missions teams have also been sent to other states. Members who go from this church prove to be strong leaders in other congregations.

Another vibrant Indian congregation is First Indian Southern Baptist Church in Los Angeles. Under the pastorship of Lewis Hancock, Choctaw, the church is doing a similar ministry as Glorieta and is growing young leadership.

In the Small Town
Spring Baptist Church, Sasakwa, Oklahoma, has always been a strong church, vitally involved in the programs of the Muskogee-Seminole-Wichita Indian Baptist Association. Services utilize both the Seminole-speaking elders and those who speak English. The pastor, George Jesse, has led the church in deep worship of the Lord, Discipleship Training, Sunday School, spiritual growth, support of the youth, tithing, and promotion of Southern Baptist Cooperative Program. The church not only reaches Creeks and Seminoles, but also others in the community who respond to Spring Church's active ministries.

Some Baptist Cherokee pastors in eastern Oklahoma saw the need to reach their people who were not coming to church. They thought one way would be through the use of radio, so there is now a weekly Cherokee radio program. Several pastors rotate the responsibility as they give testimonies and preach the word of God.

Siloam Indian Baptist Church, on the outskirts of Phoenix, has a young pastor, R. C. Falls, Sauk and Fox. He led his young people to reach out to a reservation that needed a ministry. Through the efforts of these youth, a new Indian congregation was started. Indian youth, committed to the Lord and with a burden to reach their own people, initiated a VBS and evangelistic efforts that resulted in a new church start!

Work among Native Americans needs more young people with a vision and a daring to be used by the Lord.

First Indian Baptist Church, Shawnee, Oklahoma, sits in the middle of five local tribes. This church, guided by Gary Hawkins, Creek/Cherokee, is deeply missions-minded. Missions teams and individuals have gone around the world, literally, to spread the gospel. They have gone to South and Central America, Mexico, Canada, New Zealand, Russia, and Israel. The church has sent building crews to several reservations, conducted Vacation Bible Schools and evangelistic crusades across the country, and started three churches in Oklahoma and California. Young preachers in the church were placed as pastors of these new congregations. Youth have also been involved in student summer missions. It is encouraging to see a pastor guiding his church to be vitally involved in missions.

Lumbee Indian churches from the Burnt Swamp Baptist Association in North Carolina are deeply concerned about reaching Native Americans across the nation for the Lord. Raising thousands of dollars, they have helped struggling Indian Baptist missions on northern reservations to erect church buildings. They too have sent missions teams all across the country to develop and strengthen Baptist Indian work. The association has been responsible for starting an Indian ministry in Baltimore, Maryland, and is looking to help initiate new Indian works in New England. Mike

Cummings, the Burnt Swamp Association director of missions (DOM) is one of those responsible for keeping a strong missions vision before the churches.

Missions History Yet to Be

Although there are exciting things happening with the blessings of the Lord, there is much to do. With many cities still without ministries to our Indian people, and many reservations yet untouched, it will take a cooperative effort by all of us to make an impact on the Indian missions field. I have been deeply appreciative of missions groups who have sent supplies that have been useful to small churches.

One Seminole congregation who received boxes of supplies placed the three boxes on the floor before the pulpit. The congregation encircled the boxes and gave thanks to God for the women and the girls and boys who made the supplies possible. Crayons, glue, scissors, pencils, pens, construction paper, Bibles, and so forth, often go to small congregations for their Sunday School needs. Towels, washcloths, hand soap, shampoo, toothpaste, and other personal items go to the pastor and his family—a big help to those on limited incomes.

The need for missions teams in some areas and even partnerships with an Indian pastor or missionary on the field is great. These workers need to know that they are being upheld by faithful prayers and a vital concern for their needs and ministry. What if local churches became burdened about Native Americans on the reservations and in the cities in their states and began to pray and seek the Lord's leadership? You can network with us to reach them for the Lord. We just might see revival happening and greater outreach among the American Indian than we have ever seen before. Pray with us that we will see it happen to the glory of Jesus' name.

HISPANIC AMERICANS

Gus Suarez

As I look back at my life from childhood to the present, it is very clear that God's hand is molding me. Even before my salvation, His tender touch and firm direction was there. I believe that these years were my preseminary training. It is my conviction that each of us ministers out of who we are. Therefore, I share part of my pilgrimage so that you, the reader, may better understand who I am.

I was born in Havana, Cuba, a few years before Fidel Castro took over the island. My family consisted of my parents, my sister, and me—a small and very close family. I was just starting kindergarten when Castro took over the country. My father, concerned for what I was learning, would always ask, "What did you learn in school today?" On this particular day, I described how we were told to close our eyes and open our hands while someone put a piece of candy in our palms. The teacher then asked, "Who gave you the candy?" I immediately answered, "God gave us the candy." Needless to say, we heard a lecture on how there was no God and it was Castro who had given us that candy.

My parents, as many parents of that time, began to contemplate all possible options—the fact that Communism was intensifying; that I was getting close to the age of *pionero*, the time when youngsters began mandatory indoctrination. The future possibilities for my sister and me led my parents to decide to leave the country.

The first felt impact of communism on my life came in
1961. My sister, 8 years older than me, had been my closest
friend. She left for Canada, and a piece of my life was torn
out. My father was granted permission to leave in 1963, and
3 months later my mother and I left Cuba, never again to
return. We were all reunited in Panama where I finished the
third grade. Later that year my family and I moved to
Managua, Nicaragua, where I studied in an American
school. I started my first preparation there—learning
English—toward our goal of coming to America. I learned a
new culture and met new friends.

In 1967, at age 13, I left for Virginia to study for the next
6 years at a military school. During vacation times, I was
able to visit my parents in Nicaragua, Colombia, and Chile.
My years at the military school taught me the benefits of a
disciplined life.

During my senior year at the University of Maryland I
accepted Jesus Christ. Soon after, responding to His call into
full time ministry, I attended Mid-America Baptist
Theological Seminary. After my first year there, I married
the former Diana Dell'Erba, then graduated from Mid-
America with a master of divinity degree in 1982. Diana and
I lived in Dunkirk, New York, where I served as
pastor/church starter of the Spanish Baptist Mission until
1985. The Lord called us back to Maryland in March of 1985
to serve as language catalytic missionaries with the Baptist
Convention of Maryland/Delaware. During those seven
years of ministry, we saw the birth of our two sons, Phillip
Andrew and Matthew Tyler. Since May 1992 I have served
as language missions director for the Baptist Convention of
New Mexico.

As a language missionary for the last 14 years, I can
clearly see that my training in cross-cultural understanding
started when I left Cuba and was exposed to the many different cultural backgrounds of people and countries I had the
privilege to visit. God was preparing me then for the ministry
I continue to do for Him today. To Him be the glory!

Cultural data

According to the most recent census, the United States is home to more than 27 million Hispanics. More than two-thirds of these live in the Southwest. Immigration has added millions over the years. However, some people of Mexican descent trace their origins to the early settlers from central Mexico and Spain. Some of these arrived in the Southwest before the *Mayflower* reached New England, many arriving before the US-Mexican war in 1846.[1] These early settlers called themselves Hispanics or Spanish Americans.

Hispanics come from 23 different countries. Each group is different from the other and each likes to retain its own cultural characteristics. Many names used to describe Latino communities correspond to national groupings, such as Mexican American, Cuban, Puerto Rican, and so forth. However, in this chapter, I will use the larger, all-inclusive title of Hispanic.

Expressions such as "America is a melting pot" and the idea presented in our currency *E Pluribus Unum* ("out of many, one") lead to the assumption that everyone coming to the United States will eventually blend and become an "American." This is not true. The United States is not a melting pot, but rather a nation of many nations. It is the different cultural baggages brought to the US by immigrants who have enriched and made these United States a strong nation. For example, A. P. Giannini, an Italian immigrant, opened the Bank of Italy in 1904 in the city of San Francisco. It later became the giant Bank of America. Other Hispanics such as Vicki Carr, Ricardo Montalban, Roberto Clemente, Henry Cisneros, and many more have made positive contributions in the areas of music, drama, architecture, sports, law, and public service.[2]

In this chapter I will attempt to present to you what Hispanics are like and how you can witness to them. The three primary groups, Mexican; Puerto Rican; and Cuban, will be emphasized. "Other Hispanics" include all Spanish-speaking people except the three primary ones.

I accepted the invitation to write this chapter with much apprehension, knowing of the enormous diversity among Hispanics, even the generational gaps within each group. Someone will read this chapter and come to a particular point at which he or she may say: "This is not me." It is my hope and desire to be as general as possible, yet fair in the description and presentation of who we are as Hispanics in the United States.

Above all, I trust that as you gain a little better understanding of Hispanics in the US, you will consider how this knowledge bears implications for ministry to Hispanics.

Diversity Within a Culture

Mexicans

Our ancestors were among the early explorers and settlers in the new world. In 1609, 11 years before the Pilgrims landed at Plymouth Rock, our Mestizo (Indian and Spanish) ancestors settled in what is now Santa Fe, New Mexico.[3] The number of Mejicanos in the United States nearly doubled during the decade of the 1980s. Today that population, the largest of all Hispanic groups, stands at 13.5 million.

During the 1830s, tension arose between Mexico and the United States over the control of Texas (Texas was a part of Mexico). The increased number of Anglos in Texas led to the closure of the border. This in turn escalated the conflict between Anglos and Mexicans, eventually leading to the Battle of the Alamo. Justo Gonzalez writes, "Thus in the beginning it was not Hispanics who migrated to this nation, but this nation that migrated to Hispanic lands."[4]

Other factors that influenced the numeric growth of Mexicans in the US were:

• *The Treaty of Guadalupe Hidalgo of 1848.* Mexico lost half her territory to the United States. Many of the people who had property lost their land. However, those who could read fought to retain their land and many of them did. Because of widespread illiteracy and distrust among the Mexican people, titles were legally defected without any major defense.[5]

- *The effect of US industrialization.* The industrial development period provided work opportunities in centers such as Detroit, Chicago, and Milwaukee. The numbers of Mexicans continued to increase until the Great Depression of 1930. A program of repatriation forced more than 400,000 Mexicans, many of them born in the United States, to return to Mexico.[6]

- *The "braceros" program in 1942.* After World War II, Mexico agreed to provide the United States with agricultural workers. This program ended in 1964, but it served as a catalyst in linking communities in Mexico with settlements in the United States.[7]

Today the border between Mexico and the US continues to be a controversial issue. The Mexican proximity to many of the southern states, the great masses of people wanting to cross the border, the difficulty in arresting and prosecuting, and the network of family and friends in the United States continue to encourage many Mexicans to cross the Rio Grande.

Puerto Ricans

The island of Puerto Rico was logged as a discovery by Columbus on his second voyage in November of 1493.[8] *Los Puertoriqueños* are the second largest group of Hispanics in the United States, accounting for 12 percent of that population. They have a unique relationship with the US—Puerto Ricans cannot vote in elections nor are they represented in Congress. By an act of Congress, they became US citizens in 1917. Shortly after this action was taken, a series of struggles over home rule followed. President Harding went on record as being opposed to the independence of Puerto Rico.[9] In 1948, Luis Muños Marín became the first popularly elected governor of Puerto Rico. All others before him had been appointed by the United States.

The migration of *Puertoriqueños* began in the 1900s. In 1920 the population of Puerto Ricans on the mainland was at least 12,000. This increased to 53,000 in 1930 and to 90,000 in 1944.[10] Initially there was an endless need for farm workers. During World War II, some people worked with the railroads, others in the mines in Utah, still others in a soup company in New Jersey.[11] Today Puerto Ricans live in every state of the union. However, a high concentration of *Puertoriqueños* is found in New York City.

The struggle between statehood and independence continues to be a hot issue for this group. Clara Rodríguez, in her book *Puerto Ricans Born in the USA*, shares the hurts that are equally true for other *Puertoriqueños* and concerns one must consider in ministry to this particular group.

Mexicans and Puerto Ricans in the United States are here because of the territorial expansion of past generations of North Americans. Their lands have been taken from them and annexed to the United States, and their citizens have been guaranteed rights under treaties with our government; these treaties have often been broken or ignored, and the people have been forced to conform to "American ways" to exist.[12]

Cubans

Cubans are the third largest national origin group in the United States. They numbered 5 percent of the 1990 population count. Cuba was a colony of Spain. Carlos Manuel de Cespedes led in the Ten Years' War from 1868–1878 in the struggle for independence. Like Puerto Rico, Cuba was acquired by the United States as a result of the Spanish-American War of 1898. But unlike Puerto Rico, it became an independent country in 1902. Drawn by cigar manufacturing, Cubans have been coming to Key West and Tampa since the early 1900s.

Immigration patterns among the Cubans differ from those of other Hispanics in the sense that initially they were political and not economic refugees. Another point that makes the Cuban exodus unlike others in recent times is that by 1970, Cuban communities were firmly established and highly visible in southern Florida and other northeastern cities.[13]

Other Hispanics such as Central and South Americans have their history of migration to the United States as well. But without writing about all of these, I can surmise that all immigrants, like people in general, are affected by the history they carry with them. These factors determine how they respond to others. As you and I become conscious of the unique factors of each group and individual, we can be more effective in our ministry to the *ethnos* in America.

Portrait of the Hispanic in the US
This section of the chapter is the most important and yet the most difficult. When you speak of Hispanics you are referring to people representing many different cultures and traditions. A good place to begin would be by asking the following question: Who are these Hispanics and where do they live?

According to the 1990 census information, Hispanics are a large and fast-growing segment of the nation's population. Projections estimate that by the year 2030, 59 million Hispanics may call the United States home. In the decade from 1980 to 1990 Hispanics grew in number seven times faster than the rest of the nation. Factors influencing the enormous growth were a higher birth rate than the rest of the population and substantial immigration from Mexico, the Caribbean, and Central and South America. In 1990, according to the census, nine of every ten Hispanics lived in only ten states. California, Texas, New York, and Florida are the four states with the largest proportion of Hispanics. Most Hispanics live in the southwestern states: New Mexico, California, Texas, and Arizona. The Hispanic population has a higher proportion of young adults and children and fewer elderly than the non-Hispanic population. Nearly 40 percent of Hispanics in the United States are below 20 years old and 7 out of 10 Hispanics are younger than 35 years old.

The Mystique of Family

Although some people will argue that Hispanics are no more familistic than non-Hispanics,[14] I will argue differently. The previously mentioned study failed to take into consideration the culture of the Hispanic. We are, in general, very family-oriented.

La familia is so highly valued that family well-being takes priority over individual well-being. Hispanic families are usually patriarchal; that is, authority is vested in the male head of the home. Typical of the Hispanic family is the extended family. For example, *compadres* is a strong bond built between a child's parents and godparents. *Concuño*, a word that does not exist in English, describes the relationship between the sibling of your brother- or sister-in-law and you.

The idea of *machismo* is known more as a social system based on the superiority of the male rather than a system of pride and family respect. In its best sense, it means that the man is to protect the family from danger and to defend the family's honor.

Many Hispanic cultures plan a big event for females as they reach 15 years of age. In many ways, *quinceañera* resembles a wedding. Usually the young girl wears a long white dress and the entire family attends a mass. This ceremony is followed by a formal dinner.

Hispanic families do not believe in putting their elders in a nursing home. But in the US, because of the tremendous pressure placed on the family by society, some Hispanics do not have any other option than to place their elders in a nursing home. However, this would be their last recourse. Hispanic families show affection for each other in the exchange of *abrazos*, or hugs. It is not uncommon for an adult son to kiss his parents.

Factors that have had an impact on Hispanic family life include:

- *Distance.* Some families may be separated by living in different states or even countries.
- *Work.* The need for two-income households has necessitated that the wife work outside the home.
- *Generation gap.* Children born or growing up in the US go through a process of syncretism; that is, they retain some of their cultural roots but they also gain a new culture. The combination of these two produce a cultural perspective that is naturally somewhat different than that of the parents or first-generation immigrants.

Religion

Many people equate being Hispanic with being Catholic. Indeed, the reality is that a great number of Hispanics, although not faithful, are Catholic. However, the hold of Catholicism upon the Hispanic is not based on religious belief. It has much more to do with our culture. Many facets of our life are incorporated in our religion. Baptism, celebration of *quinceañera* (or the 15th birthday for females), confirmation, first communion, marriages, and holidays are all part of our cultural loyalty.

Past immigrants such as Italians, Poles, and others have brought their priests with them thus facilitating their participation in the American church. Even in the northern pueblos of New Mexico, one can see that the main building in the pueblo is the Catholic church. One can also observe the syncretism of Pueblo and Catholic religion on the drawings in the walls of the church.

As Hispanics come to the US, they bring religious traditions as well. For example, many Caribbean people bring roots of spiritualism. In Cuba, spiritualism was used to undermine the church for generations. South Americans influenced by Gustavo Gutierrez, the father of liberation theology, bring an emphasis on the social gospel. Cesar Chavez, a Mexican, hoisted the banner of the Virgin of

Guadalupe above his marching *campesinos*.[15] The idea was that God was an active participant in this movement.

An interesting contrast is that the family is patriarchal but religion is maternalistic. Women usually dominate religious life among Hispanics. In most cases, the father is not highly religious. He may make his appearances at church only during special events. But, the mother is responsible for the religious teaching in the home.

Protestant churches have been very successful in reaching Hispanics in the United States. In the words of one priest, "Protestants do a lot of things we Catholics don't. They knock on doors. They visit the sick and pray for them." Hispanics respond to kindness. Southern Baptist success in reaching Hispanics with the gospel can be related to a few factors:

1. The personal interest shown to people.
2. Churches strongly led by laypeople rather than the clergy.
3. Language (Spanish) being the primary means of communication.
4. The very lively worship experience tied to lay participation
5. A very practical presentation of the gospel where people feel the Word will meet their everyday needs.

Education

Many Hispanics have experienced a rapid change in lifestyle moving from rural to urban areas. It has been my experience that Hispanics coming to a metropolis from a rural lifestyle do not place as much emphasis on the education of their children as those coming from South America. Census information shows that although Hispanics lag behind in education as compared to the non-Hispanic population, they have made great strides in educational attainment since 1970. Only 3 out of 10 Hispanics 25 years old and over completed at least 4 years of high school in 1970. Today, about half of the Hispanic population has received at least a high school diploma.

Our educational attainment varies among different Hispanic groups. Spaniards and people from South America lead Hispanics in educational achievements with 77 percent and 71 percent, respectively, having received a high school diploma.

Language

Spanish is the language used by these different nationalities known to us as Hispanics. It is the tie that binds us together. Spanish is clearly the second most used language in the United States. The 1990 reports show that 78 percent of Hispanics spoke a language other than English at home. However, there are variations in the use of the language as it is communicated in North America. These variations of dialect and vocabulary (among others) are regionally based as well as evidenced by the country of origin or Hispanic heritage.

I will never forget the way my limited knowledge of English was immediately put to the test when I came to school in Virginia in 1967. My frustration level rose rapidly. I thought I knew the basics of the language, yet I had never heard the southern "y'all." When a common language is shared by different countries, identical words can have different meanings. For example, *tortilla* to a Cuban is an omelette. To a Mexican or someone from Central America it is a thin, flat pancake made from corn flour. *Camión* to a Cuban is a truck, but to a Mexican the same word means bus.

Spanglish and Tex-Mex are variations (or language blends of Spanish and English) found among Hispanics in the United States. Puerto Ricans and Mexicans, respectively, receive credit for these new words. However, second and third generations in the US undoubtedly must get credit as well. An example of this hybrid language is found when someone translates "I will call you back" as "*Te llamo pa tras*," or in some cases, "I call you *pa tras*," where the sentence mixes words from English and Spanish.

Shared Struggles

Hispanics in the United States share some common struggles. Language is a problem for many of our people. It is
my observation that Hispanics are found to be Spanish
dominant, bilingual, or English dominant. The first is true
primarily among recent immigrants and people living in
communities close to the border where Spanish is the primary language. The second group includes those that are
language-equipped to live in two cultures. Of course, one
could further divide this group into bilingual-Spanish dominant and bilingual-English dominant. The third group is
made of those Hispanics who are English dominant. Among
these are individuals who can speak minimal Spanish. In
New Mexico, 38 percent of the population is Hispanic, yet
most of these Hispanics are English dominant. Others have
come to the conclusion that eventually all Hispanics will be
just like Anglos. The assumption made here is that we are
all marching toward assimilation and eventually will get
there. But I must caution that this idea is not factual. While
it is true that some Hispanics inevitably will assimilate, others will become bicultural and bilingual. These will discover
a new culture while preserving their cultural roots. Another
factor to consider is that unlike the European migration,
Hispanics will continue to come to North America. The way
our people respond to the English language will determine
their future in North America. It will either help or impede
the ambitions of the individual.

A second common struggle of the Hispanic in the US is
that of education. Ironically, language is one factor that prevents Hispanics from pursuing educational advancement.
Parents' attitudes toward education is another factor. The
rural versus urban mentality of the parents will affect their
thinking regarding education. Certainly one could think of
many other factors influencing education among our people, but the summary of it all is that Hispanics lag behind in
this area. This in turn propels us into a third common struggle—economic disadvantage.

Three facts reflecting our economic disadvantage can be noted:

- fewer of us held jobs as managers or professionals than non-Hispanics;
- our median income was $10,000 lower than that for all Americans; and
- over 1 million of our families lived in poverty in 1990.

A fourth struggle common to Hispanics in the United States is that of acceptance. Coming to the US does not necessarily mean acceptance. One can still find traces of ethnocentrism here—the attitude that one's own ethnic group, nation, or culture is superior to all others. The fact that one has an accent may lead others to conclude that the person is not well educated. The Hispanic who happens to have darker skin than others in the neighborhood could discover setbacks in some areas as well.

Ministry

The Great Commission tells us to go to the people of all the nations and make them disciples of Christ. This verse is a mandate for all Christians to reach out to people from all nationalities. As well known as this verse is, I find that people often misunderstand it. Perhaps subconsciously people think this verse means that one must go to a foreign country to reach people of different cultures. Twenty-seven million Hispanics call the United States their home. *This is a missions field!* This also means that the possibilities for confusion, frustration, and misunderstanding are present because of cultural differences. My challenge to you is to look at cultural differences as an opportunity to minister and not as an obstacle.

Getting Started

1. A genuine desire to see people come to know the Lord is a prerequisite to anything you may want to do to reach Hispanics.

2. Get to know the Hispanics in your missions field. Find
   out where they are from, what brought them to the area,
   and where they currently work.
3. The local Baptist association should be able to help you
   with demographical information concerning the Hispanics
   in your area. Other places you may be able to find help
   are: chamber of commerce; language missionaries; Baptist
   state convention or fellowship; police department; director of missions; school system; local college/university;
   military base; local Hispanic church.
4. Know what type of ministry you want to do. In other
   words, be specific rather than general.
5. Pray and ask God to open doors for ministry.
6. Get started. Do not procrastinate.

Ministry Opportunities to Consider

1. Because second- and third-generation Hispanics can sub-
   sist in the US culture easier than the first generation, I
   would like to offer outreach ideas primarily for new immigrants. Since more than one-third of the Hispanics in
   the US were foreign-born, some opportunities that will
   meet their needs include:
   - *Sponsorship*—Teaching an individual or a family about life
     in the United States; sharing your culture and food but let-
     ting them teach you about their culture and food as well.
   - *Conversational English*—Taking time to teach a group
     of new immigrants the English they need to do routine
     tasks and manage independently.
   - *Job opportunity*—Provide a job for your new friend.
   - *Immigration papers*—help families with the complicated
     legal papers they must fill out in order to apply for legal
     residence in this country.
   - *Citizenship classes*—The ultimate goal of many of these
     friends is to make a positive contribution to life in the
     United States. Some eventually decide to become citi-
     zens. You can help teach citizenship classes at your
     church or community center.

2. Because some of the Hispanics in North America are in colleges and universities, you and your church may be able to help by "adopting" a student. During vacation time many of these students cannot return to their homeland. Many students will be without any family and quite lonely at holiday times. Perhaps you can invite them to spend that time with your family.

3. Because Hispanics lag behind other groups in education, you may help by tutoring young students in your local schools.

4. Because many churches lack strong leadership, you can minister by making a commitment to training. You can join forces with the local association and/or language missionary to help train leadership from the Spanish-speaking churches.

5. Because you, the reader, may not be a Hispanic, some things that will help you personally in ministering to Hispanics are:

   • *Learning Spanish*. Take classes that are offered locally or seek a Hispanic person who will help you learn the language.

   • *Learning the culture*. Cultural awareness conferences may help you understand more about Hispanics.

6. Because the median age of Hispanics is 26, you need to consider what activities will best meet the needs of this young population. Activities dealing with parenting, education, job training, and other similar life skills are a few suggestions.

7. Because Hispanics are family-oriented, any invitation extended to our people must include activities for the entire family.

8. Because Hispanic families are patriarchal, you must reach or consider the man of the house when extending an invitation to the family.

9. For single-parent households, possible ministry opportunities might include child care or events providing support for the single parent.

Different Strokes for Different Folks

Many people today mistakenly believe that a church is for "all" people. We are starting to see a generation gap between first-generation Hispanics and their children. The 1990 census reported that about 64 percent of us were born in the United States. Manuel Ortíz, in his book *The Hispanic Challenge: Opportunities Confronting the Church,* presents a series of models to best reach Hispanics in cultural transition.

Model 1: *Growing alongside.* A church that is trying to meet the linguistic and cultural needs of second-generation Hispanics. One group will conduct worship and Sunday school in one language. But alongside that group is a bilingual, multicultural group worshiping and having Sunday school in English and Spanish.

Model 2: *Growing Within.* One church with one bilingual service and Sunday school.

Model 3: *Growing Without.* This promotes the starting of a new church with its own leadership. An example is the starting of a bilingual church to reach second and third generations from an existing monolingual church.

Model 4: *Growing Through House Church.* This model involves the entire church in an intentional approach to church starting among other groups. In our example, a Hispanic church is involved in the starting of a second-generation house church. This can be an intermediate step to get to the type of church described in model 3 above.[16]

As you can see from these models, it takes all kinds of churches to reach all kinds of people. This is true even when one speaks regarding one ethnic group.

Some Problems to Avoid

Assimilation. Do not try to make Hispanics lose their identity. Many of our seminaries graduate "Anglo" ministers in brown bodies.

Prejudice. Do not fall into the trap of speaking as a missions-minded individual with a prejudiced heart. I know of a church whose pastor really desires to start a Hispanic congregation within their church. However, one of the deacons told the pastor that he is all for a Hispanic church, but it must be outside their church.

Dependence. In a sponsorship relationship, it could be possible for the Hispanic church to become dependent on the sponsoring church. This will extinguish the flames of growth into maturity. Make use of a written plan describing the journey from beginning to end.

Expectations. Make sure that Anglo expectations are not imposed upon the Hispanics. Remember, all ministries must be contextualized to the Hispanic culture. If not, they will become nothing more than another culture's program among Hispanics. This may prove to be non-productive and self-defeating.

A Personal Word

The Book of Acts records a conversation between Jesus and His disciples. One of these men asked, "Lord, are you now going to give Israel its own king again" (Acts 1:6)? As part of our Lord's response to this question, He said: "You will tell everyone about me in Jerusalem, in all Judea, in Samaria, and everywhere in the world" (Acts 1:8). I challenge you to look for a place to minister in your Jerusalem.

Three words of counsel as you make preparations to reach out to Hispanics or perhaps other language groups in the United States. First, look up. God's Holy Word is available to you. The Bible tells us, "Everything in the Scriptures is God's Word. All of it is useful for teaching and helping people and for correcting them and showing them how to live" (2 Tim. 3:16). In 2 Corinthians 5:18–19 we read about God giving us the ministry of reconciliation. And the Great Commission assumes that we are on the go. This verse is translated in the Greek as saying, as you go make disciples of all the *ethnos.* (Matt. 28:19). All power that you will ever need comes from our Lord, so look up!

Second, look within. Before you are able to minister to others, you must look inside your own heart. Do you have a godly attitude? Do you want to be used by God to reach all people with the gospel? Most people will respond positively to someone who shows kindness and compassion. As a man or woman of God we are called to do just that. "Instead, be kind and merciful, and forgive others, just as God forgave you because of Christ" (Eph. 4:32).

Third, look around. Do you see your neighbors walking in darkness? Do they need a helping hand? Do you hear the voice of Jesus telling you, "A large crop is in the fields, but there are only a few workers. Ask the Lord in charge of the harvest to send out workers to bring it in" (Matt. 9:37–38)? One final question for you as you complete this chapter: Are you *that worker* the Lord is calling out? If you are, would you say as Isaiah did, "Here am I. Send me!"

May our gracious Lord strengthen you as you seek His will.

-----

[1]Matt S. Meier and Feliciano Ribera, *Mexican-Americans/American Mexicans,* (Canada:Harper Collins, 1993), 3.

[2]America's Hispanic, (unpublished material from Language Missions Division, Home Mission Board, 1992), 45–46.

[3]US Department of Commerce, *We the American Hispanics,* September 1993, 1.

[4]Manuel Ortíz, *The Hispanic Challenge: Opportunities Confronting the Church* (Illinois: Intervarsity Press, 1993), 45.

[5]Ibid.

[6]Ibid, 47.

[7]Ibid.

[8]Juan Angel Silen, *Historia de la Nación Puertoriqueña* (Rio Piedras: Editorial Edil, 1980), 37.

[9]Kal Wagenheim, *Puerto Rico: A Profile* (New York: Praeger Publishers, 1973), p. 70.

[10]Joan Moore and Harry Pachon, *Hispanics in the United States* (New Jersey: Prentice Hall, Inc.,1985), 36.

[11]Ibid.

[12]Ortiz, 48.

[13]Frank D. Bean and Marta Tienda, *The Hispanic Population of the United States* (New York: Russell Sage Foundation, 1987), 28.

[14]Ibid, 185.

[15]Thomas Weyr, *Hispanic U.S.A. Breaking the Melting Pot* (New York: Harper & Row Publishers, 1988), 195.

[16]Ortíz, 117–121.

ANGLO-AMERICANS

Rob Nash

Hello! I am a white, Protestant citizen of the United States of America. As is generally descriptive of other white Protestant Americans, my cultural heritage is primarily English with perhaps a little Scotch-Irish, German, and/or Scandinavian thrown in. To make matters even worse (or better, depending on your perspective) I am a white, Protestant, American male.

I spent 13 years of my childhood and adolescence in the Republic of the Philippines where my parents served as Southern Baptist missionaries. This experience provides me with a rather unique perspective on what it means to be Anglo-American.

Since I was born in 1959, I was just a bit too late to take full advantage of the so-called heyday of white, Protestant male opportunity in the United States. Nevertheless, these attributes have, for the most part, enabled me to enjoy a life of considerable privilege. Only recently have women and ethnic groups begun to challenge my status in society. Rarely have I experienced any sort of prejudice. Any and all careers were attainable for me virtually from the moment of my birth. My choice of schools was limited only by my ability to meet the academic requirements.

Most banks will loan me money and most country clubs will welcome my membership if I have the money to join. I can buy a home in practically any community in the nation.

Most people will pay attention to me if I wear a nice coat
and tie. Police officers usually treat me with respect when
they stop me for speeding. In short, I sit at the top of the
ladder in US culture.

I refer to myself as an *Anglo-American*. Certainly many
kinds of "white" Americans live in the United States, including persons of Eastern European, Italian, or French ancestry.
I have chosen to use the term *Anglo-American* to include
only persons of English descent.

I teach at a small liberal arts college. As each semester begins, I ask my students in church history classes to participate
in an activity called "confession." Most of my students are
Anglo-American. Together we identify ourselves as a group.
We recognize that we are mainly white, Anglo, Protestant,
Southern, and Baptist. I ask students from other countries and
regions and races to engage in a similar exercise.

Then I ask a question, "How are our attitudes shaped by
these characteristics?" Anglo-American students respond
with many of the same conclusions I outline in this chapter.
In the end, I remind them that we cannot help who we are,
but we can become more fully aware of our own strengths
and weaknesses and the perspectives that are dictated by
this social group to which we belong.

It is my hope and prayer that this overview of
Anglo-American culture will enable members of this ethnic
group to more fully understand themselves.

The Dilemma of Dominance

Trying to communicate the characteristics of Anglo-American
culture presents me with some unique challenges. My ethnic
group also happens to be the majority culture in the United
States. To put it another way, for many of us it is quite easy
to equate American with Anglo-American even though we
know that Americans come in every ethnic variety. I might
choose to describe myself as a generic American—but
generic brands are not predisposed to stand out! The characteristics of a generic brand of ice cream tend to be the quali-

ties of all ice creams. In the same way, the characteristics of Anglo-Americans tend to be the qualities purported to be the qualities of all Americans in general.

While we were in the Philippines, my family was part of a minority group in a majority Filipino culture. On rare occasions I experienced some of the feelings that came with knowing I was an alien in a strange land. I remember observing some anti-American sentiment as Filipino nationalists cast Molotov cocktails at the United States embassy. But for the most part I was warmly welcomed into the Filipino culture and extended every sort of hospitality. I often felt more like an honored guest than an outsider. Unfortunately, many non Anglo minorities in the United States do not receive such kind hospitality.

As a majority group, many Anglo-Americans often exhibit the classic traits of a majority group that mark our culture whether we live in the United States or anywhere else in the world! Outside the United States, we tend to view ourselves as guests who ought to be welcomed wherever we go. Our behavior suggests that we are citizens of the most powerful nation in the world. It seems clear to us that all people should welcome our presence.

We inevitably exhibit the classic traits of a majority culture in the United States. We may be hospitable toward persons of other ethnic groups. But we also tend to select the traits of minority groups that distinguish them from us and use those traits to isolate these groups from the mainstream of US culture.[1] We choose skin color, a different language, or distinctive dress as a way to show that members of other ethnic groups are "different" or "not one of us." Then we carefully isolate such people groups so that they are unable to change "our" culture. As a result, our attitudes and behavior give rise to the term *ugly American*.

For our part, such attitudes are quite subtle. We prefer to voice them only to other Anglo-Americans. I could list a whole range of statements to back up this assertion. Anglo-Americans in my town of Rome, Georgia, refer to an area

near my house as Little Mexico. In this part of town,
Hispanic families live in rented hovels which are in serious
need of repair. I have heard relatives bemoan the fact that
too many Vietnamese were moving into the state of
Georgia. Some Anglo-Americans are quick to condemn the
traditional African clothing that some African Americans
might wear during a Kwanza celebration.

These attitudes are the classic expressions of a majority
culture that is attempting to make other groups conform to its
self-defined cultural pattern. Indeed, Anglo-Americans are
quite unaware that such statements are harmful at all. For
many, this practice has worked quite well through the course
of US history. Africans, Asians, and other Europeans have
been forced to become like Anglo-Americans before they
could be fully accepted by the dominant Anglo culture.
Ironically, full acceptance into the dominant culture has been
almost impossible. However, increasing levels of immigration
have begun to change this prevailing Anglo-dominant cultural
pattern. The latest trends indicate that the Anglo-American
percentage of the US population is diminishing. Today the
overall white portion of the population stands at 73.6 percent.
By A.D. 2050 this percentage will have dipped to 52.8
percent.[2] Along with other whites, Anglo-Americans are losing
their dominant status, and thus losing the ability to compel
other ethnic groups to fit into the Anglo culture. Many other
ethnic groups are discovering new freedom to wear distinctive
dress, speak their own language, and celebrate their own heritage. Indeed, a new day has dawned.

Our Strength, Our Weakness
Ministry to Anglo-Americans is not particularly easy. We are
a proud people who believe ourselves to be self-sufficient,
highly capable, and hardworking. We are proud to be of
English and American ancestry and tend to think more
highly of ourselves than we ought. We congratulate ourselves for the great accomplishments of Western culture—its
literature, inventions, explorations, art, and overall contribu-

tions to humanity. We also are proud that it is our cultural heritage that provides the cultural core of the United States of America.

Our great spiritual problem is that we often fail to see our shortcomings as a people; indeed, we sometimes act as if we do not possess any shortcomings at all. Therefore, it is my firm belief that this failure to acknowledge our own shortcomings is both our greatest strength and our greatest weakness as a people. It is essential to understand this paradox if we are to minister to Anglo-Americans.

Why, you may ask, is this characteristic a great strength? It is a strength because it provides for me and for other Anglo-Americans the firm conviction that we can do anything we set our minds to do. We need only to look back through our history to find evidence to support this conviction. Anglo-Americans are firmly convinced that from a wilderness they hewed the greatest nation in the world. Against great odds, they turned forests into farms, landed a man on the moon, and defeated virtually every enemy.

"Wait just a minute," you might interject. "You Anglo-Americans did not do all of this by yourselves. A team effort was required. All Americans of all ethnic persuasions participated in these accomplishments."

In that, you are right!

Now we begin to understand why it is a great weakness that Anglo-Americans fail to see their own shortcomings. We are quite honestly convinced that we did all of these things by ourselves or that God did them through us. If asked directly, many of us would certainly deny this. We would insist that by "we" we mean all Americans—red and yellow, black and white (as the popular children's chorus phrases it). But we would be lying. The stark truth is, when we say "we," we mean Anglo-American!

We rarely engage in self-criticism. We rarely pause to ask the question, Where have we made our mistakes? Our optimistic confidence in our own unflagging ability to be right and do right is one of our most irritating traits.

This trait causes us to be insensitive to the needs of other ethnic groups in our communities and in our churches. Increased immigration to the United States has caused explosive growth in the number of ethnic congregations that are tied to Anglo-American churches. Yet I notice that it is rare for the Anglo mother congregation and the smaller ethnic congregation to be truly integrated. Rarely do the two congregations hold joint services. Rarely does any kind of shared community occur.

In my 13 years in the Philippines I never came across a Filipino Baptist Church with an American Baptist congregation meeting in the basement. For the most part, a church was a church was a church. We worshiped together no matter what our nationality or ethnic heritage. Yet Anglo-Americans in the United States prefer to do church with other Anglo-Americans, while other ethnic congregations live a separate life under the same roof! Why?

One conclusion might be that Anglo-Americans have little interest in true cross-cultural dialogue. Another answer might be that as the dominant culture, Anglo-Americans simply take the presence of other ethnic groups for granted. Or we may actually view other ethnic groups as a threat to "our way of life." Perhaps the correct answer is that to varying degrees, all of these responses are somewhat true.

Keep in mind that our greatest strength as an ethnic group is also our greatest weakness. Our great confidence in our own abilities as a people often leads us down the road away from interaction with other ethnic groups. It gives us a false sense of pride in our own accomplishments. It also provides a nice set of blinders which helps us live with the misconception that we built this nation by ourselves.

The Slippery Slopes of Defining a Culture

Who is a typical Anglo-American? A typical Anglo-American is virtually impossible to describe. He might be a wealthy Republican lawyer who worships at First Baptist Church or

St. John's Episcopal Church. She might be a single divorced mother with three children who must have food stamps to feed her family and whose prospects for bettering her socioeconomic status are quite slim. He might work at an electric plant and be active in a labor union. She might be an advertising executive with a major corporation who travels internationally and is involved in a New Age congregation.

Let us explore what it means to be an Anglo-American by taking a close look at four aspects of social life that all ethnic groups share: family, church, school, and community. I hope these categories will help you to understand the unique characteristics of Anglo-Americans.

Family

What is it like to be part of an Anglo-American family? Obviously, no two families are just alike. On your own, you can note many exceptions to the picture of family life I describe. Like all ethnic groups in America, the Anglo family has been significantly affected by the rise in the divorce rate, the emergence of blended families, and an increase in the number of single-parent households. Nevertheless, let me attempt a few observations about the Anglo-American family.

First, Anglo-American families have witnessed drastic changes in home life in recent decades. Economic realities have forced both parents in many homes to become wage earners. As a result, our children are often raised by child-care providers. In addition, children now spend considerably more time participating in extracurricular activities in the community than was true in the past. Mothers and/or fathers must coordinate soccer, basketball, baseball, and gymnastics practice as well as a whole range of other community activities. These realities have diminished the quantity of time parents have to spend with their children and have increased the levels of stress in the home.

Secondly, the children of today's Anglo families are much more apt to distance themselves from the community affiliations of their parents. This is particularly true as it

relates to one's denominational or religious preference.
Several different factors have influenced this lack of "brand"
loyalty. The generation of Anglo-Americans born after 1950
was raised in a consumer culture. We attend the church
which meets our needs most effectively. Today's young
adults tend to take a cafeteria-style approach to religion.
They may attend Sunday School at one church and worship
at another. They may change denominations at a moment's
notice. Tensions arise when parents and grandparents who
do have a sense of denominational or religious loyalty fail
to understand this experimental approach.

Finally, I think that Anglo-American families are rather
unique in that what we call the immediate family, or nu-
clear family, is the primary focus in the culture. We tend to
gather with grandparents, parents, and children much more
than we do with the larger extended family. This pattern
holds true as we celebrate such holidays as Easter,
Independence Day, Thanksgiving, and Christmas. Certainly
there are exceptions. But, in my own family, we rarely gathered with aunts, uncles, and cousins once the grandparents
who served as the family patriarch and matriarch had died.
At that point, parents became the new matriarch and patriarch, and their children and grandchildren gathered at their
house for the holidays.

Church
When it comes to the church and religion, Anglo-Americans
are increasingly diverse. I recently attended several church
services that illustrated the diversity among Anglo-American
congregations.

St. Paul's Episcopal Church, Philadelphia, Pennsylvania
I attended St. Paul's Episcopal Church in Philadelphia,
Pennsylvania, for its 300th anniversary. Chills ran up and
down my spine as the church resounded with the strains of
the orchestra's preservice music. Representatives of various
sister congregations carrying huge banners processed down

the center aisle, passing pews which were once occupied by such luminaries as Betsy Ross, Ben Franklin, and George Washington. The priests entered in their clerical robes and proceeded to the front of the sanctuary to deliver the sermon and to lead the congregation in the Eucharist, or Lord's Supper. I was awestruck by the central place of this church in the nation's religious history and particularly its Anglo-American heritage.

Baptist Church, Gainesville, Georgia

Here funeral parlor fans rested in the pew racks in a sanctuary devoid of air-conditioning. The preaching and worship style was informal. We sang hymns like "Beulah Land" and "What a Friend We Have in Jesus." In the middle of the service an elderly woman in the pew in front of us screamed out in a holy shout.

"Whooeeee . . . whoooeee, Lord!" she hollered, slapping me enthusiastically on the back as she danced out into the aisle. The congregation kept right on singing.

"Amen, sister," said the preacher. "You just keep that shouting up."

Unity Church, Atlanta, Georgia

Recently, Anglo-Americans have turned to a new religious movement which combines elements of Christianity, Eastern religions, and self-help approaches. A number of congregations have emerged in larger cities where middle- to upper-income Anglo-Americans seek to enhance their spiritual lives. In this particular congregation, the service blends spiritual readings and music with a short, encouraging sermon. The sacred writings of many different religious traditions may be used in the service. Church members believe in reincarnation and hold to the idea that a new age is about to dawn in which humanity will reach its full potential.

Storefront Mission, Louisville, Kentucky

This storefront mission near downtown Louisville ministers

to down-and-out street people, many of them Anglo-
Americans. The congregation is a mixed group of transients,
seminary students, social workers, and a few elderly people.
Their pastor is a woman, a seminary graduate, who is well
loved by her church members. Her ministry is carried out
among what Tex Sample has called "hard living people."[3]
Men from another local church have prepared breakfast for
those who have no place to eat. The worship service is
warmly informal. A guitarist leads a chorus. The sermon is
on Christian unity. Afterward, everyone shares in some refreshments.

This quick survey of four Anglo-American congregations
provides ample evidence that, at least on a religious level,
Anglo-Americans share very little in common. But it is important to remember that members of nearly every congregation mentioned emerged from a common English heritage.
Anglo-Americans tend to be Protestant. Our differences all
emerge from this common tradition and can be traced to ge-
ographical location, socioeconomic strata, and educational
levels. These differences result in a wide range of worship
styles and often dictate how open or closed we are to theological perspectives that are different from our own.

Community
Common notions of community in the United States emerge
from the traditions of Anglo-Americans. By this I mean that
Anglo-Americans have contributed the primary cultural picture of what life is like in the United States. Social customs,
concepts of etiquette, and community patterns of relating
are contributions of the majority culture. This cultural picture is not easily defined. It is best portrayed in Norman
Rockwell's portraits of American life and involves such
Anglo-American cultural icons as Poor Richard's Almanac;
sayings like "What's good for the goose is good for the gan-
der"; and social gatherings like a Fourth of July barbecue.

Therefore, I would like to expand the category of community among Anglo-Americans to include the notion of

"society" or "culture." For good and for bad, we Anglo-Americans view ourselves as the people who supplied the United States of America with its cultural core. Our ancestors include the Puritans of the Massachusetts Bay Colony, the Quakers of Pennsylvania, the Baptists of Rhode Island, and the Anglicans of the southern colonies. We are the people who forged a common identity out of a ragtag bunch of colonists and created a government "of the people." At the same time, we are the people who ignored this very principle of government when we relocated Native Americans onto reservations and enslaved Africans.

Several factors present among these early European settlers influenced the development of a unified culture that was predominantly Anglo-American. In the first place, the common cultural core among the 13 original colonies was English. In 1700, 70 percent of the settlers were English. Another 20 percent were Scotch, Irish, or Welsh. Five percent were African. The remaining colonists were a mixture of various other European nationalities. These settlers brought with them a common language and culture (English) and a common faith (Protestant).[4]

Secondly, these European settlers united around common enemies: namely, Native Americans; Catholics; the French; the Dutch; the Spanish; and, eventually, the English. Conflicts with these various groups resulted in the emergence of a culture which was, at heart, Anglo-American and Protestant.

From the very beginning, these Anglo-Americans were possessed by a confidence that was both strength and weakness. The Puritans of the Massachusetts Bay Colony insisted that they were on a divinely appointed mission to establish the kingdom of God on earth. In 1630 John Winthrop, governor of the colony, likened the Puritan endeavor to the establishment of "a city upon a hill, the eyes of all people are upon us."[5] Anglo-Americans appropriated this Puritan notion of divine chosenness as a metaphor for the nation. The United States became, for most Anglo-

Americans, God's great tool for Christianizing the world and for extending Western European civilization.

As the years passed, Anglo-Americans became more convinced that God's hand was upon the United States and, by extension, upon the Anglo-American people. America's successes in the War of 1812, the Spanish-American War, and World Wars I and II served to cement this conviction. The nation's superpower status through the cold war solidified the idea that God was on the side of Anglo-Americans in particular and the United States in general.

But even as Anglo-Americans celebrated their accomplishments, they virtually ignored the unequal status of African Americans, Native Americans, and other ethnic and religious groups within the nation. US history is a study in irony. The nation "of the people" has consistently resisted any effort to extend the boundaries of chosenness to include other religious and ethnic groups. Catholic-Protestant tensions erupted in the nineteenth century when Anglo-American Protestants charged Roman Catholics with undermining American democracy. Only with the election of John F. Kennedy to the presidency in 1960 did Anglo-American Protestants extend to Catholics some grudging acceptance.

In recent decades, we have witnessed the heightening of racial tension in the United States as both African Americans and Native Americans have asserted their rights to the same privileges held by Anglo-Americans. The systematic relocation of Native Americans and the enslavement of Africans are certainly an ugly blight on the Anglo-American conscience. Equality has been extended to these groups only as they have asserted their right to full partnership in the nation's political, social, and religious structures. This quest for equality has forced Anglo-Americans to gradually relinquish their tight control over their perception of the nation's cultural core.

Along with these tensions, Anglo-Americans have watched as the world has invaded the United States through immigration. Most Anglo-Americans are unsure about how to respond, but are profoundly disturbed by the forecast of their own displacement. Not long ago, I took a great aunt to a Chinese restaurant for lunch. She was amazed to discover such a restaurant sprinkled among the steak houses and hamburger establishments in her town. She was mystified by the large Laughing Buddha that dominated the restaurant's entryway.

"Is that Buddha?" she asked curiously.

"Yes, it's Buddha," I replied.

"It's a different world," she answered.

Indeed, it is a different world. New religions have been introduced from Asia as Chinese, Thai, Japanese, and other Asian immigrants have made their way into cities and towns across the nation. Increasing numbers of immigrants have spilled over the borders from Mexico and Central America causing significant growth in the Roman Catholic Church, particularly in the southern states.

The anticipation of a surrender of cultural control has caused some considerable anxiety for Anglo-Americans. I recently spoke at a church in a small town in Georgia. Church members were disturbed by a number of trends in their community, including the sudden increase in Hispanic immigrants in town and the opening of an Islamic mosque. They were virtually paralyzed about how to respond to these significant cultural changes.

It is important that I repeat the assertion about Anglo-Americans which I made at the beginning of the chapter. This ethnic group is characterized by a sense of its own superiority and chosenness among all of the ethnic groups in the nation. Anglo-Americans have always assumed that not only would the power of the United States subdue other nations but also that Anglo-American culture would triumph over all other ethnic cultures. We have always assumed that other groups would readily sacrifice their ethnic distinctives in order to enjoy the benefits of our cultural heritage. This assumption is a great spiritual problem. Understandably, other ethnic groups are put off by such attitudes, yet this is

the point at which Anglo-Americans can be ministered to by
other ethnic groups.

Anglo-Americans are now being faced with the reality
that not every ethnic group easily assimilates into the culture that we have carefully constructed over 220 years. This
realization has caused significant tension among Anglo-
Americans as our vision for America begins to fade. To help
you put this into perspective, let me draw your attention to
one of these tensions.

In recent years, Anglo-Americans have been divided by
a battle to define the future course of the nation. James
Hunter has written a book, *Culture Wars: The Struggle to
Define America,* that chronicles this conflict.[6] On the one
side are a group called traditionalists. These individuals believe that doctrine and morality are fixed truths which
should apply to all people in the world and to all periods in
human history. Many traditionalists believe that the United
States was founded upon biblical principles from which the
nation has departed in recent years. Traditionalists yearn for
a return to a glorious past in which the US was committed
to Judeo-Christian beliefs and morals. Their concern is for
moral law based upon such beliefs.

On the other side stand the progressives. These persons
believe that historic faiths like Judaism and Christianity
should be reshaped in each new generation to meet the
specific needs of the day. For them, the Judeo-Christian heritage does not consist of an unbending set of rules to be
obeyed. Rather, the call is for a pluralism and openness to
change in which the Judeo-Christian heritage is one among
a number of religious traditions that influence the nation.
Their concern is for tolerance and social justice.

Traditionalists and progressives offer two competing vi-
sions for the nation. Their conflict reveals that a major battle
is on among Anglo-Americans to control the future direction
of the nation. Traditionalists look to the past and see the
salvation of the United States in the Judeo-Christian worldview that has permeated the nation since the arrival of the

Puritans in the Massachusetts Bay Colony. Progressives look to the future and see the nation's salvation in the logical extension of the boundaries of chosenness to include all ethnic and religious groups in a kind of multicultural unity.

Ministry to Anglo-Americans must occur within the context of this conflict. The traditionalist-progressivist conflict emerges from Anglo-American fears and anxiety over the future direction of the nation. Anglo-Americans are disturbed by increasing non-Anglo immigration, the influx of Eastern religions, the shrinking global community, and other inevitable results of pluralism. Some of us resist such changes; others of us embrace them.

School

The basic tenets of Anglo-American culture have historically been passed on through the public school system in the US. In recent years, though, Anglo-Americans have found themselves divided over the goals and direction of public education. This division has occurred along the lines of the culture war described above. Traditionalist Anglo-Americans, sensing a loss of place for traditional Christian morality and American values, have taken public education to task for hastening the decline of American civilization. Traditionalists demand the reinstatement of prayer in public schools and the teaching of creationism alongside evolution.

Some traditionalists have gone so far as to remove their children from public institutions into private schools or even home schools. They hope to instill in their children the respect for the Christian faith and for traditional American cultural values that they believe to be absent in public education. Their fears can be directly traced to radical changes in public education brought on by increased immigration and recent Supreme Court decisions which have severely curtailed religious expression in public schools. Progressivists, however, celebrate these changes and believe them to be in the best interests of the future of the United States.

Keys to Ministry and Witness Within
Anglo-American Culture

The first key to such ministry is to simply understand that
power is difficult to surrender. Rightly or wrongly, most
Anglo-Americans do firmly believe that they have built this
nation into a world superpower. I think most Anglo-
Americans recognize that the benefits of US citizenship
should be extended to all ethnic groups and that religious
freedom should be available to all religious traditions. After
all, it was our Anglo-American ancestors who first penned
the words, "We hold these truths to be self-evident, that all
men are created equal."

But this realization does not free us from the natural human inclination to want to protect such rights for our own
ethnic group and our own religious tradition. We are, after
all, only human. We want to hang on to every inch of
ground we have conquered. We want the values and morals
of our particular ethnic group to pervade the world.

Once again it becomes clear that, for Anglo-Americans,
it is our strength that is our weakness. It is our power in
this culture that has become the source of our sin. We are
in a terrific struggle among ourselves over how to make
room for other ethnic groups in the nation. Paradoxically,
we want to do so without surrendering our central place in
that culture. Our tendency is to "demonize" other ethnic
groups. We make crass generalizations about the number of
African Americans on welfare. We complain that "the
Vietnamese are taking over" or that "Mexicans are lazy."

These assertions about other ethnic groups are simply a
mask for our own anxieties. We worry about jobs for our
own children given the influx of immigrants into the nation.
We reassure ourselves of our own cultural superiority by
categorizing and stereotyping other ethnic groups. In truth,
Anglo-Americans are worried that the nation will become a
much more pluralistic place and that we will lose out in the
process. Everyone else will gain something; we will be the
ones who lose.

"Oh, poor Anglos," you might say. "You've had it all so good for so long that it's about time you sacrificed something." And you would be right. But remember that it is almost impossible for a social group to surrender its power. The primary cause of the culture war may be this inability to willingly surrender cultural power. Think about it! Most US presidents have been Anglo-American. Nearly all members of the US Congress and the Supreme Court have been Anglo-American. Most state governors and state legislators have been Anglo-American. However, recent changes in US culture are beginning to threaten this political and cultural hegemony.

Cross-cultural relationships are the only means to overcoming such fears. I would encourage other ethnic groups to bridge the cultural gap by nurturing relationships with Anglo-Americans on both sides of the culture war. Such relationships are not easily developed. African Americans, Native Americans, Hispanics, and other ethnic groups certainly have many reasons to avoid a close relationship with an Anglo-American. But the avoidance of such relationships benefits no one. And, indeed, it harms all of us.

Anglo-Americans are a "service" people. I think that we sincerely want to benefit humankind through the resources at our disposal. Such "service" translates into significant ministries around the world, including missions and other forms of volunteerism. We want to help.

At the same time, it is often quite difficult for Anglo-Americans to accept ministry from other ethnic groups. We view ourselves as people who minister to others—not as people who are in need of ministry. We are a "missionary" people. We are offended by the notion that someone might try to be a missionary or minister to us. Our self-sufficiency and sense of self-worth work against us. The fact is, we are very needy. Deep down we know that our self-confidence is just a mask that hides our true feelings of inadequacy. We fear that other ethnic groups might discover that we are not nearly as capable as we claim to be.

You can minister to us at this point. Do not listen when we insist that we do not need your help. We simply do not know that we need it. Ignore the walls we build around ourselves to maintain the illusion of self-sufficiency. Your ministry to us will, in the end, be deeply appreciated.

In Retrospect

This chapter was very difficult for me to write. There is enough in it to offend every Anglo-American who reads it and perhaps many non-Anglos who read it. The picture I have painted seems, at first glance, an unflattering portrait. It depicts a people group in which some members are cocky, insensitive, mean-spirited, and full of prejudice. Such a portrait is only partially intentional. If I have erred, I have chosen to err on the side of our less-attractive characteristics. We do have a disproportionate sense of our own importance in human history. Our attitudes toward other ethnic groups are often paternalistic at best and downright prejudicial at worst.

On the other hand, we certainly have much for which to be proud. No one disputes the accomplishments and contributions of Anglo-Americans to the human race. Our spirit of confidence and self-assertiveness has been utilized to accomplish good at least as often as it has been the source of evil. Our missionary and service records are probably unparalleled in human history.

It is my firm belief that Anglo-Americans are much more needy than we want to admit. We are in the midst of profound crisis as we seek to find our way in an increasingly pluralistic world. While other ethnic groups celebrate their heritages, we are left wondering exactly who we are. We no longer have much in common with our cousins across the Atlantic. Our culture is much more American than it is Anglo, yet our "Americanness" is being called into question. Other ethnic groups want to join in our party; and even though we issued them an invitation, we certainly did not intend for them to change things around so drastically.

We who are Anglo-Americans have much to celebrate about our heritage. We also have much to confess. I pray with hope that those of you from other ethnic traditions will minister to Anglo-Americans in spite of our arrogance and our pride. You have much to offer to us. Please forgive our tendency to think better of ourselves than we ought. Always remember that this tendency is the source of both our strengths and our weaknesses.

[1]Richard T. Schaefer, *Racial and Ethnic Groups* (Glenview, IL: Scott Foresman and Co., 1990), 5.
[2]"White Population Share to Dip," *Atlanta Constitution*, March 14, 1996, 1a.
[3]Tex Sample, *Hard Living People and Mainstream Christians* (Nashville: Abingdon Press, 1993).
[4]Alden T. Vaughan, "Seventeenth Century Origins of American Culture," in *The Development of an American Culture*, ed. Stanley Cohen and Lorman Ratner (New York: St. Martin's Press, 1983), 32.
[5]Perry Miller, *Errand into the Wilderness* (Cambridge, Massachusetts: Harvard University Press, 1956), 12.
[6]James Davison Hunter, *Culture Wars: the Struggle to Define America* (New York: Basicbooks, 1991), 44–45.

AFRICAN AMERICANS

Dessie Dixon

As far back as I can remember, there has always been a cloud hovering in my memory of a world of fractured relationships, broken friendships, shattered dreams, and lost moments of pure, wholesome fellowship. We are always searching for our own sense of identity and our own special place in this world. People all around the world are separating themselves and setting themselves apart according to race, image, religion, and ethnic origin. Today it's happening in the Middle East, Bosnia, Germany, and the United States.

As I recall growing up in Birmingham, Alabama, the memories of many tragedies are still as real to me now as they were then. Birmingham, Alabama, a city and state that indeed have a special claim to fame and historical significance in the archives of the struggle for human rights in this country and around the world. Yet, in the early years, Birmingham was simply my hometown; the place where was located the house in which I lived with my mother and sister. It was the place of childhood impressions and memories like the day four young girls were killed by a bomb planted in a Baptist church; the many adult conversations I overheard about dogs, burning crosses, young black men hosed down and unjustly incarcerated by police officers; and the many times we had to be in the house before dark for our own protection.

I realize now, in retrospect, that I was both insulated and isolated by my environment. I was insulated from the day-to-day intensity of the racial inequities that existed between the White world and the Black world around me. This insulation was due in large part to the fact that I lived in an all-Black neighborhood and completed my education in all-Black elementary and high schools. On Sundays, I worshiped in an all-Black Baptist church in my neighborhood. On other days I spent my leisure time, including both formal and informal recreational activities, with other Blacks. Not only were my friends Black, but my teachers and my principals were Black also. My world was indeed a world where I was surrounded and insulated by my Blackness.

In the midst of this insulation, I was also isolated from another world in my environment. This world was white—a world in which it appeared that not only were the houses larger, but the schools and churches were larger also. It was in this world that the pleasant grocery stores and elegant department stores were located. It was in this world that my place was at the back of the bus. I recall that it was in this world that my mother worked extremely hard; always leaving home early in the morning and arriving home late in the evening with her body tired and feet aching. This world was so close upon me, yet so far away from me.

I had never really focused much on the things I had heard discussed around me as a child, nor the things I had seen through the media. But life has its awakening moments. Some of them came when one year after high school I accepted my first job at the Baptist Medical Center as a physical therapist attendant. My duties were to transport patients and assist the therapist with the patient's care. Sometimes I provided personal care. I approached all of my patients with a loving and friendly smile. Yet, on several occasions, I was denied the opportunity to assist patients because they refused help from me. Their refusal to accept my care was not based on my skills or job knowledge but because of who I was. I

knew this because they told me. Although I experienced
anger at times, I never forgot what my mother taught me,
which was to be proud of who I was and to always treat
others with love and kindness. In the face of obvious racism,
this was not easy, but I did it. After all, opportunity brings
opposition, and this job brought me plenty.

In the secular world, you almost expect unpleasant
things to happen; but surprisingly in the Christian community, I found circumstances to be far from what the Word of
God commanded of us as His children. When my husband
and I were home missionaries working in the area of
inter-Baptist ministries, I still encountered some of these unpleasant incidents. Our responsibilities involved creating
ministries where Blacks and Whites could worship and
work together. This was not easy. We soon discovered that
so many of our Anglo churches didn't want to have Blacks
attend worship with them nor did they want to join together
for kingdom causes. Yet my husband and I believed that
the work was important and of God. We moved forward,
accomplishing what we could at that time with Anglos and
African Americans who were willing to live out the true
meaning of our Christian charge.

In no way am I perfect. Each day I am becoming more
of what the Lord would have me to be, as a person and in
my relationships with people. The Word of God gives us
these words in John 15:12, "Now I tell you to love each
other, as I have loved you." God didn't say this was a
choice or an option, but a commandment, thereby requiring
effort and commitment.

One would think that these prejudices and harmful acts,
along with the slavery of our predecessors, would engender
much hatred forever in the lives of our people. I believe it
is a miracle that our race did not renounce Christianity alto-
gether. Perhaps we would have if we had not psychologi-
cally separated Christ from the root of these evil acts.
However, through our families, the preaching of the gospel,
and the intervention of the Holy Spirit, most of us were

taught love instead of hate, forgiveness instead of revenge, and perseverance instead of quitting. We endured more than our share of suffering basically because others thought their being different meant they were better. But different does not mean better.

People make such a fuss about being different from each other—in skin color, taste, beliefs, and religion. At the beginning of time, God did not make us different. He intended for us to be alike in spirit. God said, "Now we will make humans and they will be like us" (Gen. 1:26). God the Father, God the Son, and God the Holy Spirit are the same in every way. Even though they have different responsibilities, they function in unity as one. We as God's children should function the same way. We have different responsibilities in our work for the Lord, but that does not make us different in so far as our likeness to Him. His people seek not to be different but the same.

It is my prayer that as you read this chapter you will be enlightened, yet challenged to relate and minister with a true spirit to African Americans. May you come to the understanding that we are just people with desires, needs, and wants essentially the same as any other people. We desire to be loved and respected. We have the need to be cared for and appreciated, and we want to be recognized for our individuality and self worth.

Different, Yet One

A few years ago, my husband attended a Christian conference where he was the only African-American male present. Surprisingly, he shared a room with a young man from Tennessee who had no previous relationship with or positive image of African-American people. They spent many hours together getting to know one another, laughing, eating meals, studying, and praying. God allowed them to establish a wholesome relationship with each other in a very short time. At the end of the conference, the young man made a confession to my husband. His words were: "All of my life

my parents had taught me that black folks were different
from me. They were evil. The only other black person I've
ever known well was my nanny. But in one week you have
proven my parents wrong. You have made them out a lie."

God allowed this man to come to know my husband
personally and realize that there was no difference between
them. They were both men of God, born of the same Spirit,
and that's all he saw.

"All of you are God's children because of your faith in
Christ Jesus. And when you were baptized, it was as though
you had put on Christ in the same way you put on new
clothes. Faith in Christ Jesus is what makes each of you equal
with each other, whether you are a Jew or a Greek, a slave
or a free person, a man or a woman. So if you belong to
Christ, you are now part of Abraham's family" (Gal. 3:26–29).

God took the dust of the earth and formed one man.
He didn't form Eve from the dust of the ground, but from
Adam's side. When He made man He didn't form four
piles of earth, one black, one white, one red, one yellow,
and blow four breaths into each one. God formed one
body, Adam, and breathed life into it, thus breathing life
into all. To God, there is only one ethnic group—His children, His church.

After God destroyed the world by flood, He started re-
populating the world with Noah and his sons. "I am giving
you my blessings. Have a lot of children and grandchildren, so people will live everywhere on this earth" (Gen.
9:1). It seems that all seed in the world was destroyed except the seed of Adam in Noah and his sons, Shem, Ham,
and Japheth.

Although many races and cultures emerged over time, it
is important to know and understand that God did not create mankind to be divided into races. God has made all
people of one blood to dwell on the face of the earth. It
has been revealed that modern mankind began with an integrated family. People of all colors came from Noah's family, so there is no different kind of man, only different

colors of men, and different ways in which we live. We eat different foods, dress differently, and speak different languages, but we are all human beings loved by God.

Understanding the African-American Church

The African-American church has historically been the most important institution in the African-American community. Its influence reaches so far that some scholars will say that the African-American church is the African-American community. The Protestant church is and has been the most dominant force of freedom in the African-American community. When we had no lawyers to interpret the meaning of constitutional and human rights, the church was our defense. It was the one place to which we could turn when we had no other place to go. It was the place where we could find peace instead of panic, calmness to replace chaos, and serenity in the midst of stress.

The African-American church, as a sort of alternate society, was the only local human and spiritual organism where African Americans could be truly free. Denied full access to the larger culture of the United States of America, African Americans developed a substitute world where they could find identity and self-directed leadership, educate their young, and engage in social interaction all safely insulated from the racism of White America. In the past 40 years, African Americans have obviously gained greater access to all institutions of US society. However, the African-American church has not faded away.

The African-American church provides hope, love, integrity, social unity, and cultural balance. It is the place where everybody is somebody. For us, the church has converted oppression into poetry and haunting fears into hymns of faith, and has raised a praying people into a positive, conscientious people. Yes, the church is the vehicle of our hope.

The African-American church has been greatly distinguished by a dynamic and free pulpit. The preacher is not so much concerned about whether the trustees and deacons approve of his methods, but primarily with whether or not God approves. Foremost in his teaching will be the absolute belief in a Supreme God; the total acceptance of Jesus Christ as His Son, fully alive with all power; and the belief that God's amazing grace can save sinners from destruction.

Because the African-American church is so influential in its teachings, there are several stereotypical expressions about the pastor and the church that were shared with me from an Anglo perspective and which I would like to address.

Stereotype 1. "Black pastors preach a long time."
The average length of the worship service in an African-American church is approximately two hours. This is inclusive of not only the pastor's message but the total worship experience. It may consist of devotional or praise time, announcements, pastoral reflections, offerings, music, the sermon, and sometimes altar calls. Preaching is very unique in the African-American church. It thrives on the participation of the congregation. It is expected to be delivered with zest and power.

To one who is totally new to our worship experience, the sermon may appear to be a conversation between the preacher and congregation. The pastor initiates the conversation and the congregation answers with verbal confirmation and gestures. Some examples of this are shouts of praise, waving or clapping of hands, or even shouts of "hallelujah" and "amen." These say to the preacher, "I agree and your message is being received." The people, the preacher, and the word become intertwined in a rich theological experience. When the sermon takes the preacher to a higher height in the power of the Holy Spirit right before your eyes, the joy that leaps from heart to heart is inexplicable. The congregation is engulfed in the conversation with the preacher as he engages you in the sermon with questions such as, Can I get a witness?

Ain't He alright? Do you know Him? With each question
the response flourishes into a great thrust of affirmation,
signifying acceptance, support, and agreement with the
holy word of God.

Stereotype 2. "African-American preachers don't prepare.
They just get up and say whatever comes to mind."
The God-given ability to "rightly divide the word of truth" is
highly valued in the African-American church.
Consequently, preparation is also highly valued. Many
African-American preachers use extensive manuscripts.
However, some prefer expository preaching. To an outsider,
it may appear that the use of examples or personal stories is
a sign of being unprepared. Yet oftentimes it simply means
that the preacher is assuming his pastoral role with his
members. The examples or personal stories serve a dynamic
purpose in the total presentation of the message. These stories help the educated and uneducated alike to hear and
understand the message the Lord has for them that day. The
leader in his pastoral capacity has heard the problems, concerns, and hurts of his people. He uses the sermon time to
provide reflections and lessons for the people within the
scope of their life situations. To an outsider, this may be un-
necessary or inappropriate. But in many African-American
settings, this is a real and felt need. In his preaching style,
the pastor is responding to these needs as well as delivering
the message of the gospel.

Many African-American preachers focus on the skill of
retention—committing words to memory rather than using
notes or manuscripts. This is a tradition that evolved from
two factors. The first is his legacy from his African roots
which endowed him with the tradition of oral communication and memorization. The second is from his American
sojourn. For years the Black preacher was not allowed to,
nor was financially able to, enter seminaries that taught
preaching as a literal process. This, in turn, caused the
African-American preacher to simply maintain his legacy.

Stereotype 3. "Black pastors are all-powerful, benevolent dictators. Their people do exactly what they say."

In contrast, the African-American pastor is known and highly recognized more as a father figure in the church than a dictator. Although adults realize that they may be equal or sometimes older in age to the pastor, much respect is given to the pastor. In his role, he is one who shows concern for their spiritual well-being and for their welfare in all spheres of life, whether social, political, or economical. Just as Paul referred to Timothy as his son, it is common for an African-American pastor to refer to his associate ministers as his sons, especially if they were ordained under his leadership. This parental role in no way serves as a sign of abuse or belittlement to our people, but is used as a driving force of love for the development of lives and the survival of the church. While it is true that the pastor is considered one with power and authority, it would be untrue to say that everyone does what they are told, regardless of who tells them to do it.

These are only a few of the stereotypical ideas that are shared among one group about another. Stereotypes are often not pleasant to hear or pleasing to confront. Yet, to admit and face our unsubstantiated beliefs are the first steps to truth and real understanding.

It has been my goal here to introduce or reintroduce you to the African-American church, a prominent institution in the African-American community. An understanding of this institution is key in the quest to relate appropriately, witness, and minister in the Black community.

The Family

The Bible is consistent in its reference to the family as an important component in the life of a community of people. The family is, without doubt, a God-created organism. It is divine. We have only to look at a few key Scriptures to know with certainty that God created and cares for our families. "So God created humans to be like himself; he made men and women. God gave them his blessing and said: Have a lot of children! Fill the earth with people and bring it under your control (Gen. 1:27–28).

Man and woman made in the image of God are valuable. And since they are valuable, He has entrusted them with the replenishing of the earth through child-bearing. They have also been given the responsibility to rule the earth. The well-being of the family represents man and woman's accomplishment of the task they have been assigned by God.

One of the highest priorities in our churches, whether Anglo, African-American, or other ethnic group, must be the establishment of strong, united families. There is much room for growth in the family lives of all Americans. But let's look for a moment at the ills that plague the African-American family in particular.

From 1980 to 1990 the number of African-American families increased from 6 to 7 million. About half (48.8 percent) of these families are married-couple families. This represents an increase in two-parent families in the Black community from the 1970 and 1980 censuses. This rate is far lower than that of White families where 83 percent are married-couple families. The number of single-parent families accounts for 51 percent of all Black families. According to the Census Bureau, over half of all Black children (18 and under) are in these single-parent homes. In 1989, the median income of these Black households headed by females was $9,590. By comparison, Black two-parent households had median incomes of $31,757.

The Black family structure has been impacted by several trends. One of these trends is the lower labor force participation of Black males. Black males were less likely than their White counterparts to be in the labor force. If we are truthful, we recognize that racism and the remnants of racism have impacted this fact. It is still primarily true that African Americans, especially males, are the last to be hired and the first to be fired. The effects of crime and violence

against Black males and their higher rates of incarceration
also negatively affect Black family life. These variables also
contribute to the decline in marriageable males, which then
gives rise to female head-of-household families. These are
only a few of the complex, systemic ills affecting African
Americans that impact family structure within this segment
of our society.

Statistics can tell a story, but they do not tell the whole
story. Statistics provide the broad strokes of the painting,
but they often do not provide the details of the picture.
Stereotypes exist about the Black family, yet we must remember that there is no monolithic African-American family.
The African-American community consists of as many different family types as there are in any other community. To
help you understand this idea, I want to share with you
four Black family types of which I am personally aware.

Family A. This is a two-parent family with two children.
They live near a large metropolitan area in an elite sub-
urb. The father is a family practitioner and surgeon. The
mother does not work outside the home. The household
income is well over $150,000 per year. They are well-
known and highly respected in the community. The aspi-
rations of the children are high; one is a consistent honor
student. Their home atmosphere is loving and wholesome. This marriage has survived for well over 20 years.

Family B. This single-parent family has a female as head of
the household. The cause of this family separation is due
to drugs and the incarceration of the male. Three children
range in age from under 6 to over 18. This family struggled financially and emotionally due to the absence of the
father. Yet the female parent was able to move on by re-
newing her strength and sense of purpose through her
faith and the support of her church family. The household
income is over $70,000. The female is very goal-directed
and is determined to keep her family together, not allowing her circumstances to dictate her future or the future of
her children.

Family C. This is a young, single female who is a teenaged mother with a high school diploma. Her dreams of college or any further educational goals are effectively stymied at this time. As a child, she too experienced the single-parent household. Her method of economic support is through the Department of Human Services and a part-time job. Her household income is less than $500.00 per month. Her goals and aspirations are to enter a community college in order to get out of the welfare system and get full-time employment to support herself and her son.

Family D. This two-parent household includes four children—three grown and gone, one still residing in the home. They live in the metropolitan area near a large city. They are buying their own home. The male is college-educated and has a professional position in the workplace as a minister. The female is a high school graduate and does not work outside the home professionally. The annual household income is over $65,000. They both are quite involved in church-related activities, ministering and witnessing in their community. The family and strong extended-family relationships and values are a high priority.

These are not imaginary families. They are real. They are people I have known personally across the years. Let me assure you that they do indeed represent a cross-section of African-American family life. The Black family in this country can easily be a family with one parent present or two; a possible yearly income of over $150,000 or an income of less than $7,000. It can be a family whose adult members have completed several years of formal education above a graduate degree or one in which the highest formal education achieved consists of a high school diploma or less.

The African-American family is diverse. Therefore, the first step in developing positive understandings and relationships across cultural lines with the Black family is to reject stereotypical descriptions. This does not mean that we cannot rely on valuable research to provide us with pertinent information about a group of people. But it does mean that we must realize again that statistics are not the whole story. People to people and person to person are the best way to gain access to truth and effect change in any relationship.

Education and Community

Educational levels for Blacks increased during the 1980s. The 1990 census reported that 11 percent of Blacks had earned a bachelors degree and nearly two-thirds had finished high school. While these rates are a significant improvement over 1980 when only 8 percent of Blacks had a bachelors degree and a little over half had completed high school, they still lag behind the educational attainment of Anglo-Americans. The ten states with the highest percentage of Blacks over the age of 25 with less than a ninth grade education are southern states. In contrast, the states with the highest percentage of Blacks with some college education are in New England and the West.

The African-American population is concentrated primarily in metropolitan areas. The 1990 census revealed that almost three-fifths (57 percent) of the Black population are located in central cities. The five cities with the largest Black populations are New York, Chicago, Detroit, Philadelphia, and Los Angeles. In five cities, the Black population was more than half the total population. These are Detroit; Washington, D. C.; New Orleans; Baltimore; and Memphis. Ninety-five percent of all African Americans living in the Northeast, Midwest, and West live in metropolitan areas.

Services provided by many community organizations have contributed to the survival of African Americans in the United States. These organizations have worked through and with families, educators, and schools to effect positive, lasting change in the community. Hundreds of these effective organizations can be found in Black communities. Some of these are local boys and girls clubs, mentoring programs, tutoring programs, crime prevention programs, and job education programs. Yet we all know there is still much to be done. The problems of underemployment and neighborhood crime continue to be a major focus in the community.

Ministry and Witness in the African-American Community

To Christians who are serious about being change agents in the area of cross-cultural relationships, here are some suggestions to help you take this journey of ministering and witnessing in the African-American community.

Always and forever precede all you do in prayer!

- Learn about the uniqueness of this cultural group. It may be through a conference or class in your missions group, church, or association.
- Use your workplace or community involvements as an opportunity to intentionally develop a relationship with an African-American person or any person different from you.
- Even in nonministering or social situations, be alert and willing to speak against racial prejudices or injustices.
- Be sensitive enough not to tell racially directed jokes and stories or make trite comments that offend.
- Make sure that you see the person to whom you are ministering and witnessing as a person of worth.
- In planning a joint ministry or project with African Americans, be sure to assume a partnership rather than a paternalistic role.
- When working together in joint projects, don't pry. Be honest about your need to know answers to certain questions. In return, be willing to share openly when you are asked questions.
- Use community agencies and organizations as your first line of information about needs in the community.
- Churches of other cultural backgrounds can develop an exchange relationship with African-American churches that may eventually lead them in doing ministry and witnessing projects together such as evangelistic crusades;

hunger-related projects; onetime or ongoing projects at a
homeless shelter; or a March for Jesus event.

Here is a little exercise to help you as you prepare to
witness:
Imagine three persons who have the desire to minister and/or
witness in the African-American community. Which of the following persons do you feel took the appropriate action?

Person A had the desire to minister to families in a nearby
   community because it would make her feel good. She
   shared with her friends what she wanted to do and asked
   for their help. They decided to assist her in her efforts.
   They met one evening dressed in their finest clothes and
   stopped in the nearest Black community.
Person B began praying about the ministry project. She then
   proceeded to talk to her minister about her desire to start
   a ministry in the African-American community. The pastor
   listened carefully and agreed that it was an excellent idea.
   He suggested that they assess the needs and get the training and the proper support to carry out the plans. But
   person B, filled with excitement, called a group together
   and started out to minister to the Black community.
Person C remembered how important it is to have correct
   information. She went to several social service agencies in
   her town to get information about the needs in the community around her. She also remembered that Sarah, an
   African-American acquaintance at work, might be able to
   assist her. She scheduled a luncheon meeting with Sarah
   to share her honest desire for ministry and to ask her
   opinion of what to do and who could be other contacts
   for her as she proceeds. Person C also realized that
   prayerful planning is always appropriate, so she prayed
   tremendously through the entire process.

Which one of these ministering persons would you be:
Person A, Person B, or Person C?

I hope you chose Person C. Although they all had a desire to minister, it was just not enough. Desire without proper preparation and appropriate process can be detrimental. Know your motive before you start to minister!

Let Love Prevail

Take note of the Apostle Paul's words in Ephesians 2:14–15: "Christ has made peace between Jews and Gentiles, and he has united us by breaking down the wall of hatred that separated us. Christ gave his own body to destroy the Law of Moses with all its rules and commands. He even brought Jews and Gentiles together as though we were only one person, when he united us in peace."

The beginning process for Black, White, and other ethnic Christians is to redirect their focus so that the mental fog of distrust that clouds the atmosphere can be removed. We have been brought together as one by the death of Jesus Christ Who broke down the walls that separated us—the walls of hatred, of racial and cultural differences. We should not be governed by the rules of darkness when we are one in Christ Jesus.

The color of my skin has presented me with some challenging moments in my life. But being a part of the Black race is and always has been a blessing and a privilege. More important, it is a God-given gift for all of us to be a part of the human race. Until all Christians fully obey God's word, the experiences of prejudice will stalk us forever.

My religious upbringing and continued growth in my Christian faith teaches me that hate has no place in my life or my heart. I don't believe in playing the blame game when it comes to my personal struggles. I know that if I keep my vertical purpose straight, which is my relationship with God, the horizontal pressures of this world cannot throw me.

Be reminded of the words of Martin Luther King, Jr. when he was asked the question, How are you able to demonstrate such unusual grace in the face of such fanatical hate?

He answered, "Most hate is rooted in fear, suspicion, ignorance, and pride. Men hate each other because they fear each other. They fear each other because they don't know each other. They don't know each other because they are separated from each other."

The words of King are so true. Hate is rooted in fear and fear really is the attitude that keeps us from getting to know others. God has not given us the spirit of fear. Second Timothy 1:7 says, "God's Spirit doesn't make cowards out of us. The Spirit gives us power, love, and self control."

We must embrace the opportunity to get to know others of different cultures, races, and personalities, not as an impersonal group, but one by one. And when we do this, we will all discover, regardless of our ethnic identity, that we are not much different one from another.

DEAF AMERICANS

Sue Hill

I have been deaf since birth. Unlike most deaf people, I was born to deaf parents. In fact, my type of deafness—hereditary—occurs in only 10 percent of all deaf people. My husband, who is also deaf, fits the profile of the remaining 90 percent of deaf people who are born to hearing parents.

Just as one would not ask an Anglo person for information about the Black culture, the same principle also applies to the Deaf culture. Only those members of the Deaf culture who are involved in daily contacts with other Deaf people and are fluent in American Sign Language are knowledgeable of the values and concerns of the Deaf culture. Deaf people themselves are the true experts, not those professionals involved in careers dealing with deafness such as audiology, otolaryngology, deaf education, and interpreting.

In this chapter, the word *Deaf* will be capitalized when referring to the cultural and social aspect of deafness. When not capitalized, the reference relates to the audiological and medical definition of deafness.

Deaf Culture: A Paradigm

As a reader, you may be surprised to see a chapter on Deaf culture included in this book. When most people hear the word *culture*, the first thoughts that come to mind are ethnic dishes or native costumes. So you may well ask, "Is there really such a thing as a *Deaf* culture? Aren't Deaf people considered a *disabled* group rather than an *ethnic* group?"

When you consider the concept that culture is more
than just the physiological aspects of a people, or lifestyle
evidences such as native costumes and ethnic dishes, you
may then begin to recognize that culture extends beyond
our popular understanding. According to Eric Law, culture
has two parts: the external and the internal.

External culture is the part of culture that we see and
hear and taste. It incorporates acknowledged beliefs and
values. However, it is only a small part of culture. "The major part is the internal part, which consists of the unconscious beliefs, thought patterns, values, and myths that
affect everything we do and see. It is implicitly learned and
is very hard to change."[1]

Being deaf is not a condition that is necessarily deplored
by members of the Deaf community. As in all other cultures, in addition to the external part, the Deaf community
also has an internal part, a culture that involves the shared
values and beliefs of a group of people. In his book, *The
Mask of Benevolence,* Harlan Lane clarified the distinctions
between the disability view and the cultural model. The disability view holds that while we condemn the conditions
that led to the disability, we respect and affirm the value of
the life of the disabled person. This disability view does not
apply to the Deaf culture.[2] Deaf parents do not typically
find their joy at the birth of a child diminished upon finding
their child to be deaf. Both of my children were born deaf.
Whether our children would be born hearing or deaf was
not a major concern for my husband and me. In the Deaf
community, Deaf children are seen as precious gifts and
valued highly.

Deafness results from various causes such as spinal
meningitis, rubella (or German measles), side effects of
medication, progressive loss due to aging, or trauma. For
many hearing parents, the birth of a deaf child is a trau-
matic experience. Frequently, their first encounter with a
deaf person is with their deaf child. Their grieving process
is further exacerbated by professionals who emphasize the

disability view and infirmity model while ignoring the cultural model.

There was a time in our history, notably in the latter part of the eighteenth century, when Deaf people were viewed primarily in terms of the cultural model. Deaf people published newspapers and books. The need for special education for Deaf children was not at issue since nearly half of all teachers of the Deaf were deaf themselves. The teachers, both hearing and deaf, used American Sign Language (ASL). Instead of using evaluation methods and mind-sets of standardized testings or audiological tests, Deaf children and adults were described in cultural terms such as where they went to school, who their Deaf relatives or Deaf friends were, where they worked, Deaf organizations and Deaf sports in which they participated, and the types of service they rendered to the Deaf community.[3]

What intensified the perception of Deaf people as a deviant group? To the hearing society, not being able to hear is not normal. Being able to hear is the norm. So anyone who deviates from that norm is considered disabled or handicapped.

If we ask culturally deaf adults how they first acquired the label handicapped, disabled, or impaired, we commonly learn that some circumstance of heredity, of birth, or of early childhood marked the child as different from his parents and created an initial breakdown in communication between parent and child. The parents then saw this as deviant relative to their norms and took the child to the experts—the pediatrician, the otologist, the audiologist. It was they who legitimated the infirmity model. Why do they do it? Because that is precisely a core function of their profession: to diagnose infirmity.[4]

Unfortunately, this pathological view has become the primary way in which Hearing societies around the world perceive the Deaf. We are categorized according to the level of our hearing loss and/or speech ability. Labels such as prelingually deaf, prevocationally deaf, and so on are assigned to us. The modern term *hearing impaired* is another label used to describe the Deaf. It is a label that is commonly rejected by Deaf people because the use of the term *hearing impaired* emphasizes the infirmity model and focuses on the hearing loss rather than on the whole person. The idea is conveyed that the better the deaf person's hearing and speech, the more accepted the deaf person is by the Hearing society.

The "View" From Within

Understandably, the opposite is true in the American Deaf culture. Deaf people do not view themselves as a pathological group. To us, being deaf is the norm. It is a physical characteristic of our culture group, the external part. Just as skin color is used to identify a person's racial origins, so being deaf is one of our distinctive characteristics.

Frequently, the pathological view and the cultural view clash. An example of the conflicts that have arisen between the two views deals with the issue of speech. By speech, I mean the ability to speak for the purpose of communication, not a prepared public presentation. When meeting a hearing person who does not know any sign language, I have sometimes used my voice if there is no interpreter available and the conversation is more of an introductory or fact-finding nature. When the hearing person discovers that I am deaf, the person invariably says, "Oh, but you have such good speech!" and unintentionally offends me.

For a long time, I could not understand why I took offense at this so-called compliment on my speech. As Eric Law explained, "Most cultural clashes happen on the internal unconscious level—on the instinctual level where the parties involved are not even conscious of why they feel and react the way they do."[5] I realized that my attitude towards speech is instinctual and internal, and is a facet of Deaf culture.

Obviously, in the Deaf culture, speech is not a preferred method of communication. For hearing people, a deaf person who uses speech well is considered a success. The internal part of the Deaf culture rejects this perception as too narrow a view of the potential of Deaf people. The Deaf person who is a good, moral person, a good parent, a good spouse, and a good worker is valued. The ability to speak does little to underscore these underlying convictions of the Deaf person. Deaf people who speak well but who do not display good moral character are not respected in the Deaf community.

Unfortunately, the use of speech has been used as a point of discrimination. A Deaf friend of mine recently related to me her experience during a job interview for a teaching position. In the state of Texas, high school students in the public school systems may take a class in ASL for foreign language credit. Teachers of ASL must have a teaching certificate, either in ASL or in Deaf education or the equivalent. My Deaf friend had all the required certifications and applied for a position as an ASL teacher in a public high school. During the course of her interview, she was asked if she could talk. Because she responded no to that question, she was not hired even though she met all the stated qualifications. The methodology of teaching ASL requires that no speech be used in the classroom. However, because she did not use her speech, she was considered unemployable and unqualified, notwithstanding her fluency in ASL and her teaching credentials.

Response to Repression
The pathological view of deafness has long prevailed as a guide for hearing professionals, educators, and parents of deaf children. Nowhere was this perception so glaringly apparent as in the Deaf President Now movement that took place in March of 1988 at Gallaudet University in Washington, D. C. Gallaudet is the world's only liberal arts college for the Deaf. While other minority colleges had their minority groups represented in top administrative positions, Gallaudet University had never had a Deaf person as its

president. In seeking a new president, the 21 members of
the university's board of trustees (only 4 of whom were
Deaf) narrowed the selection process to three candidates,
one hearing person with no knowledge of sign language
and two Deaf individuals. The trustees selected the hearing
person over the two Deaf candidates. The board chairman
had served on the board for eight years but never learned
sign language because she was not often in direct contact
with Deaf people. She justified the Board's decision by declaring "Deaf people are not ready to function in a hearing
world."[6] The reaction of the Deaf students, faculty, and the
Deaf community at large became what is known as the Deaf
President Now movement. It was a groundswell that finally
erupted after years of repression. It was more than just a
protest over the naming of a hearing president. It was also a
response to a system that had for years determined what
was best for Deaf people. The Deaf President Now movement made known to the world that Deaf people intend to
be involved in decisions affecting their lives and well-being.

Just as the early Christian missionaries in their mistaken
zeal tried to convert the Native Americans or the Hawaiian
islanders to the white man's way of thinking and believing,
so hearing people have engaged in oppressive acts to make
the Deaf person "normal," that is, able to speak and hear.
An understanding of Deaf culture thus requires that the
hearing person willingly set aside any previous thoughts
and opinions about Deaf people and listen with an open
mind and heart to what Deaf people have to say about
themselves.

Listening to the Deaf

Unlike other cultures, the avenue of membership in the
American Deaf culture is not necessarily birth. A very small
percentage of deaf people, about 10 percent, are born to
deaf parents. How then can the remaining 90 percent of
deaf people born to hearing parents become integrated into
the Deaf culture?

Culture can be acquired through contacts with members of the culture. This means that deaf children from hearing families may be introduced to the Deaf community through Deaf adults or through other Deaf students in a residential school. For those who become integrated later in life at the postsecondary level, Deaf college programs, Deaf clubs, and social events of the Deaf community are the normal channels.

However, *attitudinal deafness* appears to be a more important criteria for membership in the Deaf community than audiological deafness. The person who is attitudinally deaf displays an acceptance, understanding, and identification with the values of the Deaf culture.[7] Thus, hearing loss is not the only criteria for membership in the Deaf community. The hard-of-hearing and late-deafened adults can access the Deaf community if they demonstrate attitudinal deafness. Likewise, membership is attainable to the hearing person who uses ASL and maintains social contact with other Deaf people.

Language is the heart of culture. Language is the means through which cultural members exchange ideas and pass down stories and folklore through generations. The language of the Deaf community in the United States is American Sign Language. ASL has managed to survive despite the attempts by many hearing people and "oral-deaf" people to suppress ASL, and in spite of the fact that education for most deaf children focuses on the learning of English. Up until the early 1970s, ASL was considered broken English or bad English. Hearing parents were counseled that the use of sign language would hinder their deaf child's speech acquisition. James Woodward attributed three reasons to the survival of ASL: (1) the oppression confronted by the Deaf community strengthened the ethnic bonds of the Deaf community and caused its members to unite more strongly together; (2) ASL uses the visual-manual channel, whereas English as a spoken language uses the auditory-aural channel; and (3) Deaf people rarely use ASL around Hearing people.[8] In conversing with Hearing people, the Deaf have used a variety of signing known as Pidgin Sign English that follows more closely the English word order. American Sign Language is closely identified with our group identity.

"ASL is at the heart of the Deaf Community. If any changes in thinking or behavior were to happen within the Community, they would have to be proposed in the language of the people of the Community. Thus, confining Hearing people's knowledge to a more English-like type of signing effectively protects the Community from outside influence—which, in turn, protects the status of ASL in the Community."[9]

While there is now less stigma attached to signing in public and ASL has gained recognition as a language, there is still much debate about the use of ASL in the education of deaf children. Proponents of the oral method continue to emphasize the child's need to appear normal and forbid the use of sign language and speech. On the other hand, the proponents of total communication encourage the use of signing and finger spelling. Unfortunately, its implementation has seldom included recognition of the language of the American Deaf community, ASL.

Still concerned with the need for the deaf child to "appear normal," Hearing professionals have resorted to developing manual coded forms of English, such as Signed English or Signing Exact English. These manual codes attempt to present English visually by signing in English word order. The theory ascribes to the mistaken notion that Deaf people have poor language skills and that using manual codes of English will improve those skills. While the concept for the development of the manual codes of English sounds very noble, in reality it has proven to be another form of paternalism and an attempt to suppress the use of ASL.

Language evaluations have focused solely on the deaf person's language development in the English language. The deaf person's language development in ASL is rarely evaluated, mainly because most educational diagnosticians do not possess fluency in ASL. Thus, even though the person may have above average ASL language skills, if he performs poorly in English, he is considered to have poor language skills. Currently, there are new programs in education called bilingual/bicultural programs that use both ASL and English and include the Deaf culture in the educational setting. We have hope that these bilingual/bicultural programs will help shift the trend from pursuing the infirmity model to using the cultural model in professional dealings with Deaf people.

Communication: Bond or Barrier

Stereotypes about Deaf people abound. Examples of a few are: "Deaf people are suspicious. Deaf people are sweet. Deaf people are loners. Deaf people are generally complacent." These generalizations are not true of Deaf people as a group. While a group of Deaf people were conversing together at a church, a Hearing woman observing the group exclaimed, "Oh, you are so cute! I love watching you all signing!"

One of the Deaf women in the group who is not known for her tact responded, "Who do you think we are? Dogs? Woof! Woof! Don't pat me on the head 'cause I might bite!"

The Hearing woman looked shocked and abruptly walked away. A cross-cultural conflict had occurred between this woman and the Deaf group. Anytime the racial and ethnic uniqueness of a group are not recognized, a conflict ensues. During the 1960s, white liberals pretended black people were just like white people with statements such as, "I don't care if a person is black or white!" Many Hearing people also pretend that Deaf people are just like Hearing people: "He doesn't look deaf. His speech is so good." The reality of this is that it strains relationships between the Hearing and the Deaf. In *Angels and Outcasts*, Trent Batson and Eugene Bergman note that Hearing people sometimes treat Deaf individuals as if the Deaf person is saint-like—reconciled to their hearing loss but determined to overcome it. Thus, the Deaf person is trapped. If he doesn't *act* like a saint, he shatters the illusion and creates contempt between his culture and the Hearing person's culture. "The hearing person would be horrified to hear that deaf people not only are not the saints he thinks they are but often have to exploit pity, have to lie and cheat, have to feign ignorance and so on, all just to get by in a world stacked against them."[10]

In a cross-cultural encounter, a catch-22 position often occurs. The Deaf person with the courage to exert his right to recognition as a person of dignity and worth is considered a troublemaker. For example, a Deaf man was employed as a professional counselor at a state agency. Despite his numerous requests that Hearing staff members consult with him personally, they continued to go to his secretary for consultation. His secretary did not help matters any, as she enjoyed the attention from the other staff members and often made decisions affecting the Deaf counselor's caseload without first checking with him. When the Deaf counselor complained that his secretary and the staff were not recognizing his authority and position, the Hearing staff members became angry and claimed he was being paranoid. Because the counselor asserted himself, the staff was forced to acknowledge his authority and position, but all this created needless friction on the job. If the counselor had chosen to remain silent, he would have remained likable, but his position and authority would have been severely undermined. For the Deaf counselor, the worst part of remaining silent, however, would have been the blow to his self-esteem.

Cultural clashes are inevitable, but a careful and honest examination of the internal instinctual part of our culture can help us to develop intercultural sensitivity.[11] The methods by which greetings are extended vary among cultures. In the United States, shaking hands, hugging, or nodding the head in greeting are acceptable behaviors. In the Japanese society, bowing is the standard form of greeting.

When members of the Deaf community greet one another, deafness is used as group identification:

The question Are you deaf? does not refer to degree of hearing. When a person responds in the affirmative, it means that he or she belongs to the Deaf social group. The meaning of "I am deaf" is similar to what natives from a particular country mean when they identify each other. Although different in many ways, their identification reveals many cultural similarities. For a minority group, that identification is crucial.[12]

In most cultures the most basic relationship is with the family. In the Deaf culture, the most basic relationship is with other Deaf people. Communication bonds families together. For many Deaf people from Hearing families, the absence of communication creates a void in their relationship as the following poem shows.

Thoughts of a Deaf Child

> My family knew that I was deaf
> When I was only three,
> And since then, fifteen years ago
> Have never signed to me.
> I know when I'm around my house,
> I try and use my voice.
> It makes them feel more comfortable;
> For me, I have no choice,
> I try, communicate their way—
> Uncomfortable for me.
> My parents wouldn't learn to sign—
> Ashamed or apathy?
> I never cared about the sound of radios
>   and bands
> What hurts me is, I never heard
> My parents' signing hands.

—Stephen J. Bellitz, *Florida School Herald*, April 1983[13]

My husband comes from a Hearing family and was
not allowed to learn sign language as a child. He grew
up feeling very isolated with very little contact with
other Deaf youth. When he entered the National
Technical Institute for the Deaf at Rochester, New York,
it was as if a new world opened for him. Many Deaf students and faculty members used sign language. Even
though he did not know any sign language, he knew he
had found the key to unlock the door to communication. He knew he had arrived home. The Deaf community, as it has for so many Deaf people, became a place
where he knew he belonged, a place of friendship and
acceptance.

Look, See, Laugh with Me

It is not my intent to paint a somber view of the Deaf culture. As a culture and language group, we also enjoy sto-
rytelling and humorous anecdotes. We poke fun at
ourselves and at others. Some of our jokes, like many ethnic jokes, do not readily lend themselves to translation.
The following joke is an example.

A Deaf man in a car approached a railroad crossing.
The crossing guards lowered and lights flashing, he
waited as the train went by. After the train went by, the
crossing guards were still not raised. Unable to cross the
tracks and continue on his way, he got out of his car and
approached a railroad official working inside the train
station nearby. Getting out paper and pen, the Deaf man
wrote, "Please but."

The punch line, "Please but," requires the listener to be
familiar with sign language. The sign for "but" is made
with two parallel index fingers pointing in opposition directions and then moved up similar to railroad crossing
guards being raised from the down position. In the joke,
the Deaf man was asking the railroad official to raise the
crossing guards by using the ASL sign for *but*, but writing
the English word.

Another popular joke in the Deaf community is an anecdote about a Deaf couple staying at a motel. In the middle of the night, the husband went outside to get something for his wife. Upon returning, he realized he had forgotten the room number. He went to his car and began honking the car horn. All the motel room lights came on except for one. Mission accomplished! He confidently headed for the unlit room knowing that it had to be his, since his wife would not have heard the honking horn.

His Promise Fulfilled

There are 2 million Deaf people in the United States. I am only one Deaf person, but in this chapter I have attempted to present an inside view that is unknown to many Hearing people. The final question we need to address is how this cultural view squares with the word of God.

Each Deaf person is a child of God. This basic tenet should underlie all contacts with Deaf people throughout the world. Successful ministry with the Deaf should focus on Deaf people as a language group with the opportunity to create an indigenous form of worship. Yet there are many Hearing Christians who view Deaf people from the infirmity model. Hearing people are not God's answer to "save the Deaf." For too long the relationship within the church between the Hearing and Deaf has existed on a vertical level, with the Hearing church functioning in a parental role and Deaf members relegated to the role of the child. Both Deaf and Hearing groups need to develop intercultural sensitivity and work toward a horizontal type of relationship where both work together as laborers for Christ.

In Isaiah 29:18, the Lord promised, "The deaf will be able to hear whatever is read to them." For centuries, Deaf people were excluded from hearing the word of God in their language. In many parts of the world, this is still true. God gave to the Deaf sign languages through which we could hear His word. God's promise to us has been fulfilled.

[1]Eric H. F. Law, *The Wolf Shall Dwell with the Lamb: A Spirituality for Leadership in a Multicultural Community* (St. Louis, MO: Chalice Press, 1993), 4–5.

[2]Harlan Lane, *The Mask of Benevolence: Disabling the Deaf Community* (New York: Alfred A. Knopf, 1992), 19–20.

[3]Ibid, 22–23.

[4]Ibid, 24.

[5]Law, *The Wolf Shall Dwell with the Lamb*, 9.

[6]Gallaudet in the News: Special Protest Issue, March 6–13, 1988, 65.

[7]Charlotte Baker and Dennis Cokely, *American Sign Language: A Teacher's Resource Text on Grammar and Culture* (Silver Spring, MD: T. J. Publishers, 1980), 54–58.

[8]James Woodward, *How You Gonna Get to Heaven If You Can't Talk with Jesus: On Depathologizing Deafness* (Silver Spring, MD: T. J. Publishers, Inc., 1982), 16–17.

[9]Baker & Cokely, p. 59.

[10]Trent Batson and Eugene Bergman, *Angels and Outcasts: An Anthology of Deaf Characters in Literature*, 3d Edition (Washington, DC: Gallaudet College Press, 1976), 4.

[11]Law, *The Wolf Shall Dwell with the Lamb*, 9.

[12]Jerome D. Schein, *At Home Among Strangers* (Washington, DC: Gallaudet University Press, 1989), 65.

[13]Ibid, 118.

CHINESE AMERICANS

Arnold Wong

It may surprise many of you who do not know me that you and I probably have a lot more in common than you think. You see, I was born and raised in the San Francisco Bay Area region of northern California. My father was born in San Francisco and my mother was born in Canton, China. To the chagrin of my traditional parents, my three older brothers, five older sisters, and I grew up as Chinese Americans—with the emphasis on the "American." While externally we were Chinese, culturally we were Americans with some core Chinese family values added in for good measure.

I came to know the Lord as my personal Savior when I was in the fifth grade. The ministry under which I came to the know the Lord and grow in the faith was one that focused on reaching young Chinese Americans who spoke primarily English. After spending time in the United States Army and getting a college degree, I practiced pharmacy for 10 years. The Lord then called me into the ministry and I came to Dallas, Texas, for seminary training. It was during this time that God taught me what I had to know in order to minister to Chinese people. For my last 3 years in seminary and for just over 7 years after graduation, I was privileged to pastor a Chinese church. I learned a lot about myself and about my people that I did not know before. Prior to coming to Dallas, my primary orientation to life was

the US culture. In Dallas, God put me in a place to learn
how to minister in a bicultural setting. For several years
now, I have been pastoring an Asian-American church
which is in fact a multicultural setting. The experiences over
the last 15 years have been challenging and invigorating.

As you read on, my prayer and hope is that my ministry
journey will help provide you with some practical help as
you attempt to reach my kinfolk for the Lord.

Coming to America

As we begin our mission together, it is helpful to understand a little bit about how the Chinese arrived in the
United States of America and how they have grown and
adapted.

The first Chinese came to the United States in the early
1800s. They were drawn here first by opportunities to work
in the gold mines and then by opportunities to build the
transcontinental railroad. The early Chinese dreamed of
making their fortunes here in the US and then returning to
China to live and raise their families. Their huge presence in
the United States caught the attention of William Speer, a
Presbyterian missionary to China. In 1852, Speer pioneered
the first North American missions work among the Chinese
in San Francisco, California. While work among the Chinese
was very difficult, a few more missions were established by
the 1890s.

In 1882, new laws were passed that significantly re-
stricted immigration. As a result of these laws, the Chinese
population in the United States declined drastically. It was
not until the 1940s that the Chinese population began to
grow again. The Exclusionary Laws were repealed.
Mainland China had been taken over by the Communists.
Unlike the first wave of Chinese immigrants, the new immigrants included many Chinese Christian pastors and
laypersons. These men and women would go on to start
Chinese churches, campus Bible study groups, and fellow-
ships wherever they settled in the US. The 1960s, 1970s,

and 1980s saw Chinese ministries starting, growing, and expanding.

Today, according to preliminary 1990 census figures, the Chinese population in the United States stands around 1.65 million, with the greatest concentrations in California and New York. If you are like me, such facts do not seem significant until you understand that over 90 percent of that 1.65 million are outside of the church. In terms of normal everyday contacts, the odds of our meeting a Chinese who is not a Christian is very, very high. Among the Chinese, there is plenty of missions work for everyone. And for an effective ministry among them, several hurdles must be overcome.

Understand the Nature of Our Diversity

One of the major hurdles to overcome is the lack of understanding of the Chinese culture in the US. As I have learned, the first step is to get a "general" understanding of the Chinese culture. This starts by adjusting the way we look at the Chinese people and the Chinese culture.

First, understand that Chinese people in the United States are a culturally diverse population because they come from different places and observe different customs. They come from all over the world—even from the United States! One of the most common mistakes is to assume that every Chinese person emigrated from China and that they are all the same. For generations, the Chinese have settled all over the face of the globe. For example, as a native of California, I am from an area that had a large concentration of Chinese from southern China. In my early view, all Chinese came from Canton. As I began to minister to more and more Chinese people, I began to meet Chinese who were from mainland China, Taiwan, Hong Kong, and from all over Southeast Asia, Europe, and Australia. As I got to know them even better, I realized they observed different and distinct customs in their homes, with their families, and at funerals, weddings, and other celebrations. Another fact that should not go unnoticed is that there are significant

numbers of Chinese who were born in the United States.
Their families may have come to the US several generations
ago, but their cultural orientation is American and their
English language proficiency is high. To minister effectively
to the Chinese we have to understand and appreciate the
fact that they are a diverse population. *All Chinese are not
the same.*

Second, understand that Chinese in the US are diverse
because they speak different languages and different dialects of Chinese. Although the Mandarin dialect is fast becoming the national language, many Chinese here have
retained their own dialects. Hence in the US, one can hear
Cantonese and Taiwanese as well as Mandarin. No matter
where they were born, many Chinese in the US speak
English, since they may have been educated in American
universities and work for American employers. In the case
of those born or raised all their lives in the United States,
they may not speak any Chinese at all, but only speak
English. I can remember a young woman in my first church
who was a Chinese from Vietnam. She could speak French,
English, two dialects of Chinese, and Vietnamese!

Lastly, understand that Chinese in the United States are
diverse because they cross all socioeconomic levels. At the
extremes are the very wealthy and the very poor. In the
middle is a large middle class. Generally speaking, high per-
centages of the wealthy and middle class have concentrated
themselves in the suburbs. The poor have congregated in
the Chinatown areas of major cities. Typically, many minorities in the US are stereotyped. When it comes to working
with the Chinese population, it is imperative that we rise
above stereotypes.

Understand What Influences Our Perspective

Another critical adjustment to make with regard to the
Chinese in the US is a change in the way one views the
Chinese-American culture. It is a quilt of Eastern and
Western philosophies and spiritual thinking. The traditional

Chinese culture has been shaped over the centuries by various teachers, intellectuals, and philosophers. The foundations of the traditional Chinese culture were shaped by Confucianism, Taoism, Buddhism, and popular folk religions which included ancestor worship and the worship of the river, mountain, and soil.

All four of these systems contribute to a set of core values that compose the traditional Chinese culture; i.e., the supreme importance of the family unit, the singular respect for elders, the high regard for education, the championing of a strong work ethic, the priority of living a tranquil and peaceful life. When devotees of the traditional Chinese culture hit the shores of the United States, they are bombarded by such Westernized philosophies and spiritual thought as rationalism, secularism, humanism, materialism, individualism, modernism, and postmodernism.

Eventually, their grasp of the traditional Chinese culture begins to mutate with each generation, becoming more and more like the "host" culture. Therefore, depending on which generation of Chinese you may be seeking to reach, their cultural attitudes and actions may vary quite a bit from the traditional Chinese culture you have come to anticipate. While you might expect all Chinese to be rather passive and subdued, you may find a significant number of them being very proactive and demonstrative. When looking at the Chinese culture in America, you should expect diversity in our sense of identity.

At this point, three general facts should stand out in your mind about Chinese in the United States:
1. The Chinese are a significant and growing portion of the population of the United States.
2. In order to minister to them, it is imperative that we understand that they are a very diverse people in terms of language, customs, and socioeconomic standing.
3. The Chinese-American culture is an amalgamation of Western and Eastern thinking.

In all likelihood, your concern is much more specific: What kind of Chinese person might I encounter as I try to minister in my locality?

To help with this, we can utilize two broad categories of Chinese as building blocks for understanding. One category is the Overseas-Born Chinese (OBC)—one who was born overseas and has now come to make a home in the US. The other category is the American Born Chinese (ABC)— one who was born in the US and sees it as home. The parents may be OBC or ABC. Notwithstanding, in each of these categories, different levels of thinking in terms of cultural identity exist and coexist.

The Overseas-Born Chinese include the

* *nonconformist,* who is content with who he is and has no real desire or ambition to become Americanized. He likes being Chinese and living in a Chinese environment. This individual probably lives in Chinatown and speaks little or no English.
* *semiconformist,* who manages to take the best features of both cultures, the traditional Chinese culture and the American culture, and apply them as he thinks best.
* *conformist,* who wants to adopt the American culture as his own, so he rejects the traditional Chinese cultural values and becomes Americanized.

With the **American-Born Chinese,** there is the

* *traditionalist,* who basically has adopted her parents' overseas culture and values, though she is here in the US.
* *semitraditionalist,* who is in a quandary and in the midst of an identity crisis. She tries to walk the fine line between the culture of her parents and the American culture, but she tends to favor doing whatever will get her accepted by her American peer group.
* *nontraditionalist,* who is fully converted to the culture of the United States.

Generally speaking, most people tend to think of ABCs as different from OBCs in that they are more individualistic, more time conscious, more impatient, more willing to express themselves, and less respectful of or sensitive to people different than themselves.

Even with the generalities I have shared with you, we can find some distinctive approaches for reaching these various groups of Chinese people for Christ. These suggestions are not exclusive to either group. As you might expect, some are applicable to both OBCs and ABCs.

For Ministry Among Overseas-Born Chinese:

1. **Build a relationship.** Try to find opportunities that will allow you to get to know them and they you. Consider this a long-term project. The goal is to truly love them and gain their trust and respect.

2. **Help them.** One way to get their attention is by offering to help them with whatever they need to get settled into the community. For example, you may assist them in finding a place to live; filling out forms; or getting a driver's license. Even taking them to the nearest Chinese grocery store would be appreciated.

3. **Be patient.** It will take time for them to understand the American way of doing things. At first, you might find yourself "on call" day and night, 24 hours a day, seven days a week. It might be wise to organize a ministry team so one individual does not bear the whole load.

4. **Show genuine love and concern.** Love is an international act. When they are sick, comfort them. Ask about their concerns and worries. They may not want to share with you, so do not pry. Let them share when they are ready. Tell them that you are praying for them and then briefly pray with them, if you can. Respect their privacy and keep their confidences!

5. **Refrain from being physical.** Americans are generally more physical than Asians. Where I serve in Texas, hugs are a normal part of a greeting or show of love and sup-

port. Generally speaking, Asians are very modest. Even
when they are in the midst of great pain and suffering,
hugs and kisses are subdued by American standards.

6. **Live credibly.** One of the greatest criticisms Chinese
people have about Christians is the level of hypocrisy
that exists in the church. You will need to work hard to
counteract those accusations with your own consistently
credible life. They will be watching and keeping score!

7. **Spend time with them.** They want to learn about the
United States. Take them to good and wholesome events
and attractions. Perhaps you could plan a fishing trip, go
to a sporting event or rodeo, or visit a national park.
When major holidays come around such as Easter,
Thanksgiving, and Christmas, invite them to share your
celebration and explain what the observance means to
you. The events don't always have to be associated with
church or have some spiritual significance.

8. **Answer questions.** They will have many, many questions. Be prepared as best you can. If you cannot answer
their questions, be sure to find someone who can.

9. **Be careful.** Always respect them and their ways. At times
we may inadvertently make a joke that would embarrass
them and hurt their feelings; e.g., about the way they
might dress, what they eat, their names, the way they
talk. You may consider it in good fun and they might
smile, but they remember and they do get hurt.

10. **Trust the Lord.** Try not to be pushy. Let God prepare
their hearts and let Him lead you as to when it is the
right time to share the gospel. Ask God to help you lead
them to the right person to help share the gospel with
them.

For Ministry Among American-Born Chinese:

1. **Build a relationship.** The first thing you want to do is
establish a good solid relationship that will build trust between yourself and them.

2. **Take the initiative.** Seek them out, showing them that you value them and seek to be with them. If they were introduced to you by a friend or family member, bring that person along with you for the first visit to help break the ice and enhance the comfort level.

3. **Meet in a neutral place.** Take them out for a meal at a place they would enjoy. ABCs are usually more willing to meet you in a public place for the first time, rather than in their apartment or home.

4. **Be casual.** When you do meet with them, dress and be informal. Instead of having them address you by your official title, use your first name. In my case it would be Pastor Arnold.

5. **Remember their names.** ABCs are both surprised and delighted that you remember their names. It shows interest and some degree of care and concern.

6. **Start large, go small.** When doing ministry with ABCs, start with a large gathering or event first. They can be noncommittal and choose to just observe. A sporting event or a large group of people going out together to eat is a good event. As their comfort level rises, you can get ABCs into smaller groups and/or events. As they begin to feel accepted, they will open up and respond.

7. **Be ready.** Be ready to answer questions clearly, concisely, and courageously. Because of their Westernized orientation, ABCs like logical answers that are well thought-out and presented. They are not shy about confronting issues head-on, so be ready for some disagreement. Some verses to keep in mind are 1 Peter 3:14–15.

8. **Be there!** This means not only on time when you have planned to do something but also be there when they face crises in their lives. Your presence should speak well of your promises. While they may be less than perfect about keeping appointments and promises, you need to be prompt and present.

9. **Use the Bible.** The ABCs grow up in a world that says there is no truth. You need to show them what is truth

and where you found it. What we are asking them to believe and do comes from God and not from our own
opinions and thoughts.
10. **Stay informed.** We live in a technological-informational
world and ABCs are aware of this. Therefore we in the
ministry have to stay abreast of the latest developments
on many different topics—from the latest news and
headlines to the latest models and developments in gad-
getry. It is hard, but you'll need to stay informed in order to carry on a conversation and determine mutual
interests.

In conclusion, please remember that there is a vast open
field for ministry among the Chinese in the United States.
To be effective, one has to appreciate the sheer size of this
group of people in terms of numbers. One has to understand that they are a very diverse population and strive to
understand their culture. It is my prayer that your ministry
will flourish under the power of the Holy Spirit and a little
help from the suggestions presented here. May God prepare
people and hearts for your ministry among my kinfolk.

KOREAN AMERICANS

Augustine Kim

When I came to Houston in 1967 to attend the University of Texas Dental Branch as a freshman, there were only about 300 Koreans living here. Seeing a Korean was a rare occurrence. There was no Koreatown, not even a Korean grocery store. So when Gene and Dorothy Douthitt formed a Bible study group for Koreans in Houston 2 years later, I was eager to attend. They had just come from Pusan, Korea, where they were medical missionaries. They returned, realized there were no Korean churches, and thus started a Bible study at South Main Baptist Church. I was not a Christian then, but the thought of being with other Koreans was sufficient reason for me to attend. I do not remember what I learned in the Bible study, but I remember how I looked forward to attending.

After graduation and service in the military, I returned to Houston to start a general dental practice. By 1978 the Korean population had grown to over 10,000 and more were arriving. This was due to the oil boom and Houston's key role in the oil and chemical industries. My dental practice was mainly for the Koreans who came to Houston for jobs. Some were limited in their English fluency and thus looked intentionally for a Korean dentist with whom they could freely express their problems. Also, well-educated Koreans with PhD and MD degrees came to Houston as the city continued to expand.

After I became a Christian, I looked for a place to serve. Seoul Baptist Church asked me to join them and teach the young adults. This was a congregation of about 140 adults and 60 children, with all the adults born in Korea. The church had just finished building an auditorium and had a great vision of many new members. Teaching the adults using an English curriculum translated into Korean was my assignment for 6 years. Because the curriculum was written by an Anglo author, I had to contextualize the content for the Korean students.

In my spiritual journey, God had placed an important educational training period at this time. My desire to study the Bible further led me to enroll at Southwestern Baptist Theological Seminary's Houston Branch. Though I had to attend some courses at the main campus at Fort Worth, I was able to take most of my courses in Houston and graduate with a master of divinity degree in 1994. I was in my middle 40s when I enrolled, yet I thoroughly enjoyed more than 3 years of seminary training. In fact, after one semester I asked my wife to join me in studying the seminary courses. Attending classes together was so much fun. Helping each other study and prepare for examinations at our age was much more enjoyable than when I was attending college 20 years earlier. Having fun contains a special element if it is done because of one's own desire, not as a requirement.

Currently, I serve as a part-time church consultant for the Union Baptist Association in Houston. In the Houston area, there are nearly 50 Asian Baptist congregations with at least 11 languages; 14 Korean and 10 Chinese congregations lead the way. I serve to assist them in different ways: church starting and program implementation such as Sunday School or Discipleship Training. Six Cambodian congregations are each being shepherded by pastors who do not have seminary training. I teach them and the key leaders the seminary extension program. They are so eager to learn. All of them hold jobs that range from refugee assistance to doughnut shop operation. Some must get up at

3:00 in the morning. It humbles me just to see their commitment to learn to be better pastors.

I also served as the interim pastor of First Indonesian
Baptist Church. When the pastor died, a replacement was
difficult to find. Because of my relationship with the previous pastor and my role as their consultant, the church
asked me to be the interim pastor. God's marvelous guid-
ance put us together and we have tremendous love toward
each other. The members are mainly Chinese who lived in
Indonesia. I am assisted by my wife who is also a graduate
of Southwestern Seminary.

My dental practice occupies my time for three days a
week. My wonderful staff allows me to concentrate only on
treatments while they take care of other management areas.
Another dentist treats patients while I am not at the office.
On any given day, I can see patients from all different parts
of the world: Russia, Poland, and France of Europe; Kenya,
Nigeria, and Uganda of Africa; Ecuador, Colombia, Peru,
and Argentina of South America; Mexico, Nicaragua, El
Salvador, Costa Rica, and Guatemala of Central America; as
well as Japan, the Philippines, China, Taiwan, Singapore,
and Indonesia of Asia. I marvel that God's hand is in all circumstances, even in a dental office. His kingdom is represented wonderfully there. I can be a missionary to every
tongue and tribe without taking a step from my office.

Culture Bridges the Generation Gap

As I sit in my dental office and scan the patients waiting for
treatment in the reception area, I see people of all races.
Hispanics, Asians, and Caucasians are all in the same room
waiting for their names to be called so that they can receive
treatment. As in any dental office, they seem a little ner-
vous. Some look out the window, some are busy reading.

The ones that read must choose materials. A Korean
mother intently reads the Korean newspaper that reviews
the events happening in Korea. Her face looks serious; she
may be reading something applicable to her relatives back

home in Korea. Her child, a girl of about eight, is reading a children's book written in English. She seems content just being next to her mother, in spite of waiting in a dental office for treatment. A young Hispanic boy is flipping through an English-language children's magazine and talking with his mom in Spanish.

As I see these people, I can almost read their lives; not only because I have gotten to know them personally as my patients but also because of their ethnic backgrounds. Every language group brings its own unique culture. Houston, Texas, is a metropolitan city where almost the entire world is represented. It is also a city where Asians and Hispanics are growing in significant numbers.

As I have lived in the United States for nearly 35 years, I have seen many changes. The generations change and the differences between parents and young children are obvious. The hair styles and fashions change and even the style of language changes. But the basic culture they bring does not change too much. As I treat Koreans, there are differences between the ones who just came from Korea and the ones who have lived here for a while. Even the young people show differences; the children sometimes speak Korean words that were not around a few years ago. Though there are variations, still the fact remains that they are Koreans and there are unique features in Koreans that will remain always the same.

Korea: A Brief History

The Korean Peninsula extends southward from the northeastern section of the Asian continent. It is approximately 1,500 miles north to south, with China and Russia on the northern border. Following its liberation from the Japanese occupation in 1945, Korea became a divided country in 1948, with North Korea under Communist rule. The Korean War in 1950 sacrificed many lives and brought the country into the international spotlight.

As the nation emerged from the ruins, much foreign aid poured into Korea, especially from the United States.

Missionary activity also flourished and the fruit of their ministry with God's provision has been remarkable. The first Protestant missionaries arrived in Korea in 1884. They established churches, schools, and hospitals. The first Southern Baptist work began in Korea in 1949, right before the Korean War. This followed a visit from Baker James Cauthen, then Foreign Mission Board Secretary for the Orient. He explained to the 1949 annual assembly of the East Asia Christian Church who Southern Baptists were and what they generally believed. This group voted unanimously to change their name to the Korean Baptist Convention. From then on, the Korean Baptist Convention steadily grew. Korea is a missionary-sending country as it, too, sends out numerous missionaries throughout the world.

Even though the rapid growth of Christianity is well known, the country still remains a predominantly Buddhist country. Buddhism is a highly disciplined, philosophic religion that stresses personal salvation through the renunciation of worldly desires. This avoids rebirth in the endless cycle of reincarnation, and brings about the absorption of the enlightened soul into Nirvana.

Shamanism, spirit or nature worship, is also quite common. It is based on the belief that human beings are not the only possessors of spirits. Spirits also reside in natural forces and animate or inanimate objects. The shaman is an intermediary with the spiritual world and is considered capable of averting bad luck, curing sickness, and assuring a favorable passage from this world to the next. Korean shamanism includes the worship of thousands of spirits and demons that are believed to dwell in every object in the natural world, including rocks, trees, mountains, and streams, as well as celestial bodies. One of the important aspects of Korean shamanism is the deep belief in the soul of the dead. The shaman is expected to resolve conflicts and tensions that are believed to exist between the living and dead. This belief still persists in Korea today. Nowadays, a shaman is almost invariably a woman.

It is clear that most Koreans have already been exposed to the concept and existence of deity, or a supernatural being. Throughout their lives they have seen monks and temples (often these are in mountains where tourists visit), or shamans seeking blessing from spirits and asking help in blocking evil spirits. Korean folklore frequently mentions the spirits of evil and good and of the ancestors. Many Koreans make an annual pilgrimage to the tombs of ancestors in order to worship their spirits.

The tumultuous political background of Korea has made this people group place survival above all else. Sandwiched among the superpowers of China, Russia, and Japan, Korea was often stepped upon by these countries as they tried to conquer each other. In a way, it is reminiscent of Israel's circumstance as the superpowers of Egypt, Assyria, and Babylon crossed the Jewish land in order to conquer each other. The latest occupation of Korea was by Japan, with Korea freed only when Japan lost World War II to the Allied forces. But Korea endured and is now one of the leading nations in Asia, in spite of being a divided country. Korean automobiles are exported to the United States. The country is famous for its textiles, shipbuilding, and even electronic products such as computers.

Koreans in the United States
These hardworking, industrious Koreans are now a part of the cultural mix in the United States. Their admirable work ethic has earned them a good reputation. They do not mind the difficult hours, hard labor, or even the danger that goes with being in certain businesses. They come determined to survive in the new land; and history proves that they are indeed succeeding. It does not take long for many Koreans to move from their apartments to a house.

It is not uncommon for Koreans living in the US to prioritize business above any other concern, including their spiritual condition. Because many have already been exposed to different religions in Korea, the message of the gospel is generally known. But making the commitment to accept Jesus Christ as their personal Savior or live the lifestyle of a disciple sometimes comes second to maintaining their business. Aside from having a salaried position, most Koreans are involved in businesses that open six days a week, or even seven. Their lives revolve entirely around the business, leaving home early, coming home late exhausted, only to repeat the process again the next day.

More than anything, Koreans need friends—people who will accept them and love them. Though most Koreans arrive at their destination city with some contact already established (mainly relatives), some come with mere rumors of good job opportunities in that city alone. This is the reason Korean churches play such an important role in helping immigrants adjust to US culture. Church members take care of everything including finding apartments, getting driver's licenses, getting Social Security cards, admitting children to schools, and so forth. It is obvious that with the enormous needs of incoming Koreans, the task of a local pastor is strenuous, in addition to his everyday functions as a pastor.

As you approach Koreans in the United States, it is necessary to understand their present circumstances. Most tend to be blue-collar workers. They may be operating a convenience store, either as owners or managers, working long hours. If they own the store, they may come home just to sleep. Their children are practically left to themselves to take care of the households. Often the oldest child takes on the homemaking responsibility. Schoolwork and extracurricular activities are often neglected. Similar situations can occur with those who own dry-cleaning businesses—another common venture Koreans choose. The hours are long, and often husband and wife take shifts in coming home to take care of the children.

For these hard workers, genuine friendship is like an oasis in the desert. The warm extension of love of any sort is desperately needed; if done in the name of Christ, it would be appreciated even more. Because of their experience with

Christianity and having some understanding of it, Korean
immigrants themselves may not be Christians, but they
know what Christianity stands for. Offering them help in the
name of Christ can generate instant friendship in most situations. Once trust has been built, the Holy Spirit will present
many witnessing opportunities.

Koreans are a collectivistic people (in contrast to the individualistic nature typical of Western culture. They are fam-
ily-centered, choosing to identify with a group rather than
foster their own individualism. Families unite and the bond
is strong. This also explains the crucial role the father plays
in a family as he is looked upon as the leader and the deci-
sionmaker. This aspect of Korean culture should be understood before witnessing takes place. The father's conversion
to faith in Jesus Christ will generally mean the whole family
will come to the church the following week. But when
other family members become Christians first, they may face
difficulty in coming to church without the father's approval.

Koreans prefer interdependence over independence;
they value friendship and cooperation. They value themselves as people of character and they expect agreements to
be fulfilled. Their culture requires them to maintain good
reputations. Bringing any shame to oneself or one's family
is one of the worst situations that could happen.

Open Doors of Ministry to Koreans
With Families
The most immediate concern for Koreans living in the
United States is their families. Though they are preoccupied
with their businesses, Koreans in general are highly concerned about their children's education. As a result, most
Korean children excel in school within a few years after
they arrive. Parents often gladly endure hardship to make a
living in the US so their children will benefit by receiving a
better education. In Korea it is not uncommon for a family
to sacrifice everything, even their property, to send their
child away to get a higher-quality education.

Inviting a Korean family for a meal in your house is a demonstration of genuine friendship. In Korean culture, sharing a meal is significant and inviting someone to your own home means even more. Korean society is built around families. Thus when you invite the whole family, this may rank as the highest respect you can give them. Many Korean families may never set foot in the homes of people of other cultures in the US. They cluster around their own people and never extend beyond that sphere. But they are always eager to make friends with others, and in fact, if some do have American friends, they readily and proudly share with their friends. Often their embarrassment because of their poor English-language skills or lack of familiarity with US culture prevents them from taking the initiative in establishing friendships with other cultures.

However, if a friendship is solidly built, this can lead to many other areas of relationship. They will have numerous questions to ask, struggles to share, and advice to seek. You will be considered expert in whatever area they ask about, and they will treasure every bit of advice you give. Just as Anglos in foreign countries feel lost, so do Koreans in the US. Of course, the opportunity to learn English will be welcomed anywhere, anytime. Many Koreans have little confidence in their English skills and struggle to communicate in the language. Being able to pronounce words correctly is always a major task for Koreans. The Korean language does not have phonetic equivalents for the *f* or *v* or *th* sounds. Koreans have difficulty in correctly pronouncing *r* and *l*. Careful instruction in the proper pronunciation is always welcomed.

Koreans also appreciate being invited to different events or places that familiarize them with the culture. As their social lives are often limited, any event outside of the home can be an adventure for them. Invitations to games, picnics, even amusement parks can mean a delightful day for them, and certainly children will enjoy the outing immensely.

Don't be surprised if Koreans bring you gifts or express their appreciation in some way for what you are doing.

Koreans are very proud people, and they want to let you know how appreciative they are in every possible way. Sometimes receiving gifts may be embarrassing to you, but it is an expression of their gratitude and it is all right to accept them.

The presentation of the gospel will mean so much more when accompanied by acts of Christian love. I have heard many stories of a Korean becoming a believer because of the love shown by the host family or by an American friend. When Koreans are lonely and in need of assistance, help offered in Christ's name is the best demonstration of Who Jesus Christ is. The opportunity to witness will come in many ways, including invitations to your church functions. An English-language Bible can be used as the text for studying English. Most importantly, Koreans need to see your willingness to help them because of your faith in Jesus Christ.

In Churches
Korean churches have one universal problem—they don't have enough English-speaking teachers. Most Korean churches are shepherded by pastors who came over from Korea, and their congregations consist of first-generation Koreans. This causes difficulty in finding teachers who can read and teach the English curriculum. As I serve in Union Baptist Association, I have numerous requests to provide English-speaking teachers for Korean churches, especially for the youth. This is because the children are still young enough to understand Korean and behave relatively well. On the other hand, the youth present the teacher with questions. They are in a stage of life beset with many needs that must be addressed. A first-generation Korean finds it difficult to try to answer the youth in English. Offering your assistance with English to any Korean church may result in churchwide acceptance and appreciation.

Korean youth in the United States are experiencing the "third culture" dilemma. Their parents are Korean, but they feel more comfortable with the US culture. They have to

live in two different worlds, one at home and the other outside. These youth face psychological as well as spiritual issues that must be dealt with, and it takes mature Christians
to help them meet the challenge. Often the position of
youth leader in a Korean church is filled by whoever can
speak the most fluent English, as most churches cannot af-
ford to have a minister of youth. The youth leader may not
be capable of handling complex problems. Demands on his
own life may not allow him time to minister either. Some
Korean churches must look beyond their nationality for an
English-speaking minister of youth. However, as second-
generation Korean seminary graduates begin to serve in this
area, this need may be met by Koreans themselves. As of
yet, this is not common.

Youth ministry in a Korean church may consist of teaching a Sunday School class or leading a worship service.
Because their primary language is English, the youth generally do not attend the adult worship service, which is conducted in Korean. With limited time and resources, the
pastor concentrates on adult ministry and the youth are often left out. This is a situation with tremendous potential for
witnessing. Just because they have been attending church
with their parents, no one can assume that the gospel message has been presented properly and the youth were given
chances to accept Jesus as their personal Savior. In fact,
they may have more questions if they have been in church
for very long. Even the ones who profess to have accepted
Christ as Savior as children still need discipling. Frequently,
Korean youth stop going to church once they go away to
college. Basic Christian discipleship is an urgent need in
providing a foundation to prepare the youth for college.

With School-aged Children
Helping school-aged children can be a starting place for
evangelism. This could be viewed as a wonderful opportunity to train your children to witness. Korean children
have the same needs as all human beings—the need to be

accepted. Often they face discrimination (albeit subtly), and they struggle to adjust to an unfamiliar culture and language. Having your children extend their friendship by inviting them over to your house after school and spending time together will mean so much to them. Children are especially sensitive about being part of a group and want the security of having friends. You can be the "parents" who provide what their biological parents cannot give: someone who speaks perfect English, who can help them with their schoolwork, and who will offer them American snacks such as cookies. The single greatest frustration on the part of Korean parents is that they cannot help their children with schoolwork. Their English is often poor, and learning enough English to use at work is already a challenge. Going through their children's books and assignments is a difficult task. So your offer to help their children with schoolwork will be highly appreciated.

When you decide to invite your children's Korean classmates to your home, be sure to visit the parents first to ask permission and explain what you are going to do. These parents are like any other parents—they have natural fears of what might happen to their children. Greeting the parents with a warm smile and introducing yourself shows respect for them and can gain their trust. Use wisdom in deciding how long the children should stay at your house. While the children are with you, it is better not to ask them too many questions that relate to their family. Concentrate on treating them well and showing your love for them. Maintain contact with the parents and find ways to help them.

Sometimes speaking with the teachers of the Korean children to whom you are ministering can give insight on how you can help. Most teachers are sympathetic to the difficulties of immigrant students. Coordinating school activities for the children will allow you to help the children greatly. You will also receive their parents' appreciation.

Your own children will see firsthand the action of witnessing as your family prays for these Korean children and offers hospitality in obedience to Jesus Christ. Koreans in general are very sociable people who cherish friendships and commit themselves to these relationships. Even children know the value of this, and having your children befriend their Korean classmates will mean so much as the newcomers adjust to the US lifestyle. Inviting Korean children to attend your church with your children usually will be accepted by parents if the family is not already attending a church. Parents place a premium value in their children's education. They know the value of spiritual education and are usually aware of the good reputation of teachings from Christian churches. These parents all share the same concern as any other parents in that they do not want their children to fall into trouble and associate with the wrong kinds of friends. Inviting Korean children to come to your church and picking them up Sunday morning may turn out to be the highlight of the week for those children.

In the Community
Most communities have at least a small Korean population, even rural cities. Houston has around 20,000 Koreans of all ages, and there are many opportunities to help all of them. In Houston, there are two excellent English teaching programs offered by Baptist churches. South Main Baptist Church started the Smiles program designed to teach English to foreign-born adults. Along with Tallowood Baptist Church, they are having excellent results. This kind of program attracts Christians and non-Christians alike who desire to improve their English while simultaneously enjoying fellowship. The adults meet on weekday mornings while their children are in school. This becomes not only a language learning center but also an opportunity to learn about Christ's love as they learn about US culture.

Local public schools can offer plenty of areas in which you can serve. Almost all schools have foreigners who need personal attention, especially in learning English. Volunteering your services to your school districts can lead you to a school with many Korean students. You may not be allowed to teach the Bible at the school, but stating your position as a Christian will plant a seed of interest that others may harvest later.

Hospitals are another area where volunteers are always needed. Visiting Koreans in the name of Jesus will mean so much as they are generally lonely and often confused. Local courthouses can be another place where Koreans need someone else on whom they can depend. Being in a court can be a frightening experience for anyone. So having someone who can understand what is going on can be of great help to a Korean. The juvenile department of the local police force may direct you to problem youths. If they have Korean youths in custody who need personal care, the officers will welcome you. Because this situation will involve heartbroken parents, your ministry to the youth may give you an opportunity to minister and witness to the whole family.

In Your Neighborhood
The good old-fashioned idea of being a good neighbor is still one of the best ways to witness. If you have neighbors from Korea, they need time for adjustment. Women, in particular, if they are not working, would want every opportunity to get together with you. Teaching them how to cook local dishes, how to shop at grocery stores, how to find coupons in newspapers, and teaching them English are activities that are genuinely appreciated. Although some may dispute this, it is generally true that women become friends quicker than men and learn a foreign language faster. Korean women have a bottomless hunger to learn everything about the United States.

When Korean children have to come home and stay by themselves, offer to keep them at your place until their parents come home. This is an excellent opportunity to minister. Korean parents, like others, feel guilty about leaving their children by themselves, being unsure of what the children will do. Providing a safe Christian environment for these children is a marvelous testimony of your faith and may mean a golden opportunity to witness to the children.

If you are gifted in sports, automobile repair, garden work, or other such skills, your willingness to share your expertise may mean a tremendous blessing to your Korean neighbor. Korean national sports are baseball and soccer. Almost everyone plays these sports and most Koreans are quite good. Courses such as music and art, which are normally electives here, are required subjects in the Korean school system. Koreans are well educated in these areas and most students play musical instruments. Korea is primarily an agricultural country and many Koreans are familiar with planting and generally have green thumbs. The opportunities to help them are endless.

Called to Be a Testimony

Because I have been living in the United States for years, I have taken many things for granted. But my firsthand experience when I travel to unfamiliar places shows me that simple things such as visiting grocery and drugstores can be difficult. Not only do I not know where they are but neither do I know the quality of the different stores, their specialties, reputations, and so forth. Just getting around the city and knowing what streets to use to get to a particular destination becomes a challenge. If I go to a foreign country where language is a barrier, the problems are compounded tremendously. That is how Koreans feel when they come to the United States. They face the challenge of a new culture with the knowledge that their entire savings are often at risk as they sell everything and come here. In purchasing a business, most of that money is spent and their lives literally depend on the efforts of the first few years. What better time is there than *now* to minister to their needs so that they see the love of Christ in action?

God has called each of us to be a testimony of Jesus Christ. The faith that saves is trusting Christ as Savior and is never meant to be left alone. It always seeks opportunities

to witness and demonstrate the example of Jesus Christ. God
has brought the ends of the world to our doorsteps. We can
obey the Great Commission and actually be missionaries to
the world as we lead Koreans to the saving faith and knowledge of Jesus Christ from our homes.

As technological progress continues, it seems the pressure for time keeps on increasing. Even though modern gad-
gets are made so that we may save time, we seem to have
less time than ever before. But seen from an eternal perspective, finding opportunities to expand God's kingdom
and continuing to do what Jesus Christ has entrusted us to
do should be foremost in our minds. As we face the shrinking world through media and computer science, God has
placed a wonderful people from Korea in our land. They are
here with the determined purpose of learning the language
and culture. But this is a tall order for anyone. They need assistance and support from others. Christians can offer this
love and assistance to Koreans in their time of need.

Koreans have endured much in their history. They have
a proud as well as scarred heritage. But God has been working in Korea and it is now one of the leading nations in the
world in proclaiming the gospel. God's hand is among
Koreans, and they are now coming to the US for a better
life. God may be using your hands and homes to continue
His work in ministering to Koreans. Befriending them and
offering hospitality in the name of Jesus will bear much fruit.
Koreans are a gracious people who cherish friendship, but
because of their reluctance to express their emotions openly,
or because of their fear of how you might respond, they
may not share what is in their hearts.

The Apostle John wrote in 1 John 4:11: "Dear friends,
since God loved us this much, we must love each other."
The love mentioned in the Bible always includes action, not
just mere feelings. If God prompts your heart to love the
Koreans in your circle of contacts, God may be calling you
to reach out to them in His name and share the blessings
which He gave to us. Listen to your heart.

A Potpourri
of Peoples

From its early days of habitation by the aboriginal peoples (ancestors of today's American Indians), the territory now known as the United States of America seemed destined to become a mix of the world's inhabitants. Archaeological evidence in the Southwest and the Mississippi River Valley attest to the fact that the people who were given the name American Indians called this land home thousands of years before the colonial powers decided to stake their claim.

Power struggles between Europe's explorers—the Spaniards in the early 1500s; the French in the late 1600s; the Dutch and the Russians (Alaska in the mid-1700s)— eventually resulted in victory, of sorts, by the British. Their successful hold on the 13 colonies that later became the United States of America was the culmination of one kind of expansion for this nation.

The perseverance, political shrewdness, and military prowess that increased the US holdings to 50 states and a few territories throughout the world contribute to the glory about which we sing at our patriotic events. Such greatness was built on the backs of more than the few who initiated the shift from colonial holding to international power. Millions of people from every continent found their way to these shores in the succeeding centuries of our existence as a nation. Some came because of their political connection

to the US; others were brought against their will; many
came seeking a dream fulfilled; others sought the opportunity to make a new start in a growing economy; and still
others for a multitude of different reasons. This influx of
people and purposes has contributed to the strength of the
US, for in this amalgamation of humanity is a giant web of
relationship that connects the world to the US.

The implications are great for ministry to the various
peoples and cultures within and without our society.   The
culture groups collected in this chapter are a few of those
who are able to provide guidelines for ministry to their people. What we learn from them is a small key to unlock the
doors of communication, not only to the diversity within
our fellowship, but also to a kaleidoscope of possibilities to
reach all segments of our nation with the gospel.

Ele Clay
Lampasas, Texas

Historical documentation gathered from 1996 Encyclopaedia
Britannica, Inc.

Greek Americans

As a young man out of high school back in 1969, coming to the United States from Greece put me in a whole different environment. First of all, I was away from my family for the first time in my life. Coming from a community where I knew people in the neighborhood and had friends and relatives around me all the time, I felt that all those connections were cut and that no one could fill the vacuum that was created.

As a Greek in the United States, you generally consider yourself to be someone who has come from a country with a tremendous amount of history, the bedrock of democracy. The city of Thessaloniki, half an hour north from where I was born, celebrated its 2,000th birthday in 1987. Alexander the Great left that area and conquered territories all the way to the Middle East and India, carrying with him the Greek culture. It has been reported that in a remote area of Pakistan, there is a tribe who are descendants of soldiers of Alexander the Great. They have a form of a dialect that is close to classical Greek and the people still believe in the 12 gods of Greek mythology. In 1997, all of Greece celebrated Thessaloniki— the European Union's cultural capital for a year.

Roots are very important to Greeks, as they deal with a very long past that has given shape and form to the Western world. Family bonds, despite all the tremors that have shaken these fundamental relationships, continue to be strong. In some cases, among Greeks in the US, family ties actually are stronger than in Greece because the Greek family in the US is trying to survive and keep its culture and identity. In a study I conducted about 11 years ago at Harvard University, one of the key concerns for Greek families in the Boston area was the welfare of family relationships as they were impacted by society's values and trends. The more the "Greekness" of the family—meaning both parents were of Greek descent—the greater the perceived threat from the dominant society against Greek ideals and customs.

Greeks are very fond of education; and the fact that in
the United States some of the top scientists, educators, and
academicians are Greek should come as no surprise.
Parents are constantly encouraging their children to be involved in extra academic activities, to acquire musical skills,
and to compete in appropriate areas for excellence and dis-
tinction in the communities where they live. Obtaining a
scholarship for college due to achievement is like a jewel
that the family wears proudly because of their child. Even if
the child does not get much financial aid at college, it is not
unusual for the parents to work an extra job to do something to help their child concentrate on his or her studies.
Their purpose is to alleviate the added stress of their child's
working and prolonging the years of formal study.

Greeks have also produced many individuals who have
been in civic life in the United States, serving their communities as elected officials. From the town level to the county,
state, and national levels, Greek men and women are very
much a part of the fabric of public life in the US. Greeks
are involved not only in the political affairs of the US but
they are aware of and eager to assist other US citizens. They
want them to understand something about Greece and how
that system of government is related to what we have in the
US. Some of the foundational aspects of democracy stem
from the Golden Age of the city-state of Athens in the
mid-fifth century B.C. Many times and especially over the
last 2 years, the Greek community in the United States has
rallied around Greece during its difficult times as national
interests have been threatened by neighboring countries.

For the last 2,000 years, national conflicts in Greece and
the struggle for survival in that strategic part of the world
have created a craving for exploration, immigration, and
venturing into the unknown that has challenged the borders
of history and geography every time the opportunity was
given. From the quest we learned about in Homer's *Odyssey*
to today's attitude about going overseas, Greeks have gone
all over the world to find a better way of living, to start

something in an area where they perceived their traits or skills to be in demand. Statistics tell us there are 11 million Greek people in Greece and about 10 million outside of Greece in all continents of the world. Current estimates have the Greek population in the United States around the 2 million mark.

If you were to explore the effect of this kind of movement and rationale, you would find that most of the Greek people in the US first found jobs working for someone else for a short period of time. Then they went out on their own as self-employed professionals and expanded what they learned. Greeks are survivalists and entrepreneurs; highly competitive and restless until the next stage of improvement to their businesses. They are not easily persuaded by formulas and status quo to stay within an established norm. They are willing to learn from others in order to work on their own. Although it has the drive for excellence, this highly individualistic spirit can also be counter productive when cooperation is needed.

One of the most significant aspects of the Greek culture is the connectedness that exists between one's identity as a Greek person and a Greek Orthodox at the same time. Ninety-nine percent of the Greek population is Greek Orthodox. The rest is Protestant, Catholic, and Muslim. To the average Greek person, ethnic and religious identity go hand in hand, regardless of whether or not the person has any spiritual inclinations. Only 2 percent of the Greek population attends church with any regularity. The question about someone being a Christian is considered irrelevant, since almost every Greek would consider him- or herself as Christian, having been baptized as an infant in the church.

One of the strong points in the Eastern Church is the fact that the doctrine of the Triune God, the historicity of Christ, His virgin birth, and bodily resurrection have never been disputed or debated on a denominational level. When talking with a Greek person, the idea of asking him or her to come and join another church is not the issue. The focus is on upholding one of the strong points mentioned earlier regarding the person and salvation work of Jesus Christ and how this person relates to these truths on a personal basis.

Another key aspect of ministry and witness is to be willing to listen to the person and try to comprehend what is his or her understanding about God's love and His relationship to us. It would be wise to begin from that point to help the person understand what the Scriptures say about our relationship to God and the pivotal role that Christ has in our lives. In order to lead the conversation to that point, you must have established a relationship with that individual in which genuine care and transparency are part of the person who is ministering. Being a real friend, a person who shows the love of Christ in your life and is willing to minister with no strings attached, goes a long way in challenging anybody to see the gospel actualized and lived out. Remember that Greeks are not impressed by how well you know the Bible but by the way you are living it out, how that impacts them and spills out in your relationship to them.

Ignatius Meimaris
Boston, Massachusetts

Haitian Americans

As I thought of my experiences as a black Haitian woman in the United States, this verse came to mind, "From one person God made all nations who live on the earth, and he decided when and where every nation should be" (Acts 17:26). Because of sin, mankind has forgotten this fact and lives with many walls of division. Jesus said that we should love God and our neighbor. He commanded the disciples to love one another. Christians have the responsibility to remind the world of man's brotherhood and common heavenly Father.

I came to the US more than two decades ago with my husband and four children. They were from 3 to 12 years old. We spoke very little English. Most of the time, we could only smile as people kindly addressed us. We lived in Camden, South Carolina. There, we joined an African-American church. The members did not encounter foreigners often, but they made us feel at home. My husband taught and worked as the chaplain at a Christian school. Our experiences among the mostly white staff were very positive. They seemed to genuinely love and support us.

This was not the experience of my three boys among their peers at school. There they faced various forms of racism. They came from the homogeneous culture of Haiti and now had to struggle to adapt to the pressures of a new heterogeneous one. They faced subtle forms of racism early on with betrayal from white friends, and more substantial forms when store managers called the police on them to question them for lingering too long while shopping. Because of these types of incidents, we sought to make our home a sanctuary, a place of comfort and joy.

I learned that the expectations of American women differed significantly from that of Haitian women. The attitude of men toward women in Haiti is more traditional. Men seek to assert their control as the head and chief of their households. Whereas here, it seemed that women are encouraged to challenge traditional roles. Young men and women in Haitian society did not usually assume an independent role until marriage.

As the dorm teacher at the school where my husband taught, I had the opportunity to spend time with and observe young American women firsthand. Many of the things these young women did would be considered very decadent in Haitian culture. Their loose behavior with young men in public as well as their comportment made a strong impression on my understanding of youth culture in the United States. I was determined that these values would not become the values of my children. We sought to make sure

that our children kept the religious and cultural values that
we had in Haiti.

Of course, it was easy to idealize the Haiti we left
when we encountered the imperfections of the US.
However, I had the opportunity to return to Haiti recently
after 22 years. My husband and I spent two months in
mission service there. I encountered many of the negative
things I had found in the US. I barely recognized the
country that I found.

What I do recognize in both the US and Haiti is the way
God is working to build His church. In that endeavor, I
have been specifically blessed to have witnessed how
Southern Baptists have served the world and shown love
through missions. Indeed, some of the best experiences I
have had here in the US involved working with my husband here and in Haiti through the Florida Baptist
Convention. As others come to this country, I pray that they
are blessed not only to receive from our churches but also
to be able to actively participate.

Nathalie Balzora
Jacksonville, Florida

It has been my experience that people in the United States
often assume that someone with an accent or a different
culture is inept, ignorant, helpless, and lacking in social
skills. Also, there is a tendency among the US bureaucracy
to lose patience when trying to provide assistance to a foreigner because the American assumes that the foreigner is
beyond help because of a language barrier.

Thankfully, there is empathy for Haitian women who
are struggling to cope in a different culture and learning to
speak a different language. Unfortunately, along with that
there is discrimination. For example, landlords are reluctant
to give a leasing contract to a single, foreign woman who
may also have children. She is also more likely to be taken
advantage of by attorneys and other businessmen.

I feel that in the United States everyone is free to worship in his or her own manner. I found here a refreshing attitude toward religion. In these unstable times, people seem to appreciate the spirit of religion.

Christians in the US showed me a great deal of love and respect. They seem to have a true spirit of fellowship. I always feel welcome in their churches. My relationships with these Christians have been a wonderful opportunity to experience the abundance of Christianity in US culture. My children were involved in all activities at the First Baptist Church of Pompano and were active in other English-speaking churches as well.

Haitian children in the United States are being reared with a mixture of both cultures—at home they eat Haitian food, speak Creole, and answer to parents who adhere to the Haitian culture. At school and at play, they are totally Americanized.

It's pretty hard to keep your culture in a child's heart when all he hears from his friends is the ease of the life in the US: dating, shaving legs, rock music. Children seem to mature much quicker here in the US and teenagers are much more independent.

Personally, I was well educated in my own native language (French), which enabled me to secure a professional position at the beginning of my life in the United States. I worked in the hospital as a nurse and used numerous skills to learn English. I began to recognize that many English words were the same in French, only with different pronunciations. I tried to understand the slang instead of only the formal English. From the slang I learned the attitude of the people. As I understood the attitude of the American people, I learned from their culture and passed on some of my own culture to them as well.

Learn about my people, about my culture. Don't only watch the news or read the local newspaper and believe that what they portray is Haiti in its entirety. Haiti has a rich history filled with heroes and amazing stories. Be flexible

about our way of life. We Haitian Americans want to benefit
from your knowledge, but we don't want to sacrifice our
identity.

Raymonde Dumornay
Margate, Florida

Romanian Americans

I write this perspective of ministry from the small angle of
my window: This means, from the knowledge I have in
my own experience and the lives of those around me, and
from the lives of my Baptist brothers and sisters who are
settled now in the United States of America.

For most of the people across the ocean, the United
States still has the aura of the beautiful dream, the dis-
tant golden shore, the unique land of freedom and opportunity. Our grandparents arrived in the US after the
long journey on ships arriving at Ellis Island, New York,
with their glittering eyes fixed upon the Statue of
Liberty. Their grandchildren now arrive in about ten
hours at airports in Chicago, New York, Los Angeles,
Atlanta. But their journey has the same tedious path of
dreams and tears.

Today, in almost every large city of the United States,
there is a Romanian community with people who sacrificed
much to get here. The price was high—surviving the dan-
gers of crossing the border illegally, being caught by the
Communist guards, beaten and imprisoned, then trying
again and again; or years waiting for the proper visas; or
months in the emigration camps in Italy or Austria; or having the family torn apart by years of separation. Actually,
the challenges for immigrants never end—a new country
with new laws, a new language, new jobs, new customs.
We are like children learning to live a new life. In the

process, we not only change homes and clothes, lifestyle and jobs, we actually change ourselves.

At the beginning of the century, large groups of Romanians came to the northeastern parts of the United States, where more jobs were available and industry was flourishing. The first Romanian Baptist Church was formed in Cincinnati, Ohio, in 1910, with 48 members. The first Romanian Baptist Fellowship (we call it Association) was organized in 1913. The Fellowship grew to about 14 churches at the peak prewar time in 1940. Romanian churches were situated mainly in the North: Detroit, Cleveland, Chicago, Gary, Warren, and Akron.

The second stage of Baptist work among Romanians in the US happened after 1967, with the new wave of immigrants. Although Romania's borders were closed to the West, little by little individuals and groups of families were able to escape through the Communist curtain. At the same time the Southern Baptist Convention became more active in missions among the ethnics in the States.

Today, the Romanian Baptist Fellowship also has 25 vibrant churches spreading its mission in Canada and Australia. New churches were formed in Atlanta, Georgia; in Hollywood, Florida; the Los Angeles area; the San Francisco Bay Area; Modesto, and Sacramento, California; Portland, Oregon; Seattle, Washington; Denver, Colorado; Hickory, North Carolina; and Dallas and Houston, Texas. The total membership of the Romanian Baptist Fellowship exceeds 5,000.

Most of the churches in the Romanian Baptist Fellowship use the Romanian language in their Sunday Schools and worship services. The members of our churches are part of the new wave of immigrants, not completely separated from their homeland, but not entirely Americanized.

A new generation of Romanians also exists among us— those born here in the States. They are still attached to our churches, although most of them have never been to Romania. The link is through language, family, and community ties, and extensive participation in church life. For these, being part of an ethnic group is a beautiful and rich heritage that they would like to keep. Using the energies of our youth, our churches have large choirs, well-trained orchestras, and many children's programs incorporated into the worship services.

Still, because of the present language barrier and cultural differences, we feel sometimes like islands, separated from the rest of the Baptists in the US. This is compensated for by a strong relationship between the Language Church Extension Department of the North American Mission Board and the leadership of our Fellowship. What we may consider as handicaps, the language department takes as an opportunity and channels them for enriching the vision of the English-speaking churches. This gives us the assurance that we are not alone, that we belong here.

As Romanian churches, we receive many visitors. Our ethnicity is itself an attraction. The accent in our language lends a different harmony to American English. Also, to many visitors, our church activities bring back to their minds the old ways—prayer meetings in which the entire congregation takes part; a lot of participation from the congregation; youth and children together in the worship; simple biblical sermons.

We also emphasize that both morning and evening services on Sunday are important. At one time, the Communists wanted to eliminate evening services. Baptists raised their voices in protest and the government reacted with much persecution, so the Sunday evening service is dear to us.

Romanian churches have large choirs, brass bands, orchestras, and youth choirs. We like to highlight the festive spirit, the praise aspect of our worship to God.

Living in Two Worlds
One peculiar facet of Romanian culture in the US is the fact that we live in two worlds. In a certain way, our hearts are still in Romania. News from Romania is special to our ears.

We send help to those still in Romania. We feel their joy and pain.

With the new freedom in Romania following the revolution of December 1989, new opportunities were opened for Romanians in the States to help their parent churches in Romania. Without a doubt, help for Romania was impressively channeled through many different agencies and missionary societies in the last years. However, as a unit, Romanian churches and the Romanian Baptist Fellowship have done their share. Assistance included:

- Thousands of Bibles and New Testaments shipped from the US to churches in Romania and to the Baptist Union in Bucharest.
- Romanian Christian literature sent to Romania.
- Relief packages with clothes and medicine.
- Financial help in rebuilding churches in Romania.
- Continued emphasis on radio ministry.
- Monthly financial help for pastors in rural areas of Romania, Yugoslavia, and Soviet Moldavia.
- Computers, printers, and software for churches in Romania which give them the capability of expanding the work of the printed word inside Romania.
- Help for the orphanages and the Christian schools.

The Benefits of Partnership

The impact of our churches upon Baptists in the United States may be summarized in three directions:

- Through our contributions, financial and spiritual, to local associations, we are bringing our energies together and are uniting with all Baptists in witnessing about Christ to all nations. The local associations have received us graciously as members and partners in their work. Some of our new missions have started as missions sponsored by English-speaking churches. As the Romanian group grew, the parent church grew also, and the benefits were reciprocal. With this arrangement, financial help for Romanian church starters was available from local churches or associations.

In the last several years, some churches have organized groups to travel to Romania. Partnership with churches in Romania helped them enlarge their vision.

- Through our presence, we bring a note of diversity and beauty. We are, as the King James Version says about all Christians, "a chosen generation, a royal priesthood, a holy nation, *a peculiar people*" (1 Peter 2:9). And with our accent, we *are* peculiar!
- Through our concern and work for our own people back in Europe, we enlarge the awareness and the missionary vision of Christians.

We should be the eyes of Christians. We have seen in the vast plains to the north . . . in the morning sun, the smoke of a thousand villages, where no missionary has ever been.

We should be the ears for Christians. We have heard the cries from afar, "Come to Macedonia and help us!"—be this Macedonia in Europe, Africa, South America, or Asia; in our neighborhoods in Brooklyn, or on Stony Island, or Marquette Park.

With all these, Romanian Christians in the United States and everywhere are becoming a strategic vanguard of missions, work, and vision in the kingdom of God.

Valentin Popovici
Morton Grove, Illinois

Russian Americans

What is it like to be Russian in American society? This is not an easy question to answer. In my understanding, many Russian immigrants in the United States go through quite different experiences of adapting to a new environment. Their interaction with their new country may have different levels and different stages. It can mean the acceptance of a larger culture or its rejection. Therefore, I respond to this question relying only on my personal experience and on the experiences of my immediate circle.

My experience of being a Russian in the US has been a positive one. From my first days in the US, I felt a warm welcome. I am a product of relationships between the US and the USSR. People in the US generally are happy and optimistic, whereas in Russia this attitude is lacking. Soon after I arrived in the US, I attended one of our denominational colleges where Christian values and acceptance are taught. My college years provided an excellent foundation for seminary training, pastoral ministry, and denominational service.

Besides school, my interaction with the *real* world initially was limited. I tended to spend more time with my immediate family and Russian friends. In a sense, I became an outsider without planning to. I still cherish my Russian heritage and clear cultural differences, although I no longer maintain the semi-isolation of the early years. I believe that I am extremely fortunate in many ways because I think my experience in the US is quite different from other immigrants in this country.

Characteristic traits of my culture

Russians are very social people. They like to spend time together in church with friends and family. For most Russians, socializing with each other is the most pleasurable part of their leisure time. Individualism is often viewed as negative or unacceptable. Russians are also very emotional people. In many life situations they may prefer emotionalism to cold rationalism.

The family, including the extended family, is also an important part of Russian culture. Family members tend to stick together, helping each other in times of trouble and providing encouragement on a daily basis. That is the norm.

Protestant missionaries find it more difficult to minister to Russians today. The setting has changed. The Orthodox church, relying on its heavy historical heritage, has become

more and more powerful. Many Russians today are in
search of self-identity. They are trying to redefine what it
means to be Russian. As a result, the Orthodox church is
viewed as an integral part of Russian heritage which must
be reckoned with and maintained at any cost.

Missionaries, in order to be successful, have to do their
best to maintain Russian cultural traditions. It is important
for them to be sensitive to the problems of Russia today
without demeaning the pride of its people. To be successful, a missionary ought to see the difference between *evangelizing* and *westernizing*. Failure to recognize this
difference will yield very limited results.

Anthony Ahaev
Fresno, California

Ukrainian Americans

For Ukrainians, the United States of America is a land of opportunities. We consider living in this country a great privilege. However, the first years as immigrants are
characterized by struggles and hard work—learning a new
language; getting used to the new environment; and adapting ourselves to the new way of life. In addition, we have
to go through the healing process of being separated from
our loved ones and being left with practically nothing.

Immigrant Snapshots

For new Ukrainian immigrants, it is relatively easy to find
jobs because they are ready to work in any kind of decent
job. Most of them adapt easily to the US way of life.

Aleksandr, risking his life, escaped from Communist
Ukraine 12 years ago. He obtained political asylum in the
United States. He did not have any relatives or friends in
this country. He got a job at a hospital as a technician. In

Ukraine he was a surgeon. In his free hours here in the US, he studied English diligently. After 5 years of intensive studies, he passed the exams and his diploma as a physician was revalidated. Today he and his family are enjoying the American life. In this country he found freedom, hope, and opportunity. Most of all, in the US he found new life in Jesus when he accepted Him as his personal Savior. Not only did he find in this country a better physical and material life for himself and his family but also a new meaning of life in Jesus Christ. Now he is actively serving people in their physical and spiritual needs.

Oksana came to the United States as a refugee 6 years ago. In spite of the limitation and persecution from the Communist government, from her early years she was active in the Baptist Church in Ukraine. She was able to finish accounting studies and get a government job. Miraculously, God opened the door for her and her husband to come to the US. When she arrived, she knew only a little bit of English. Immediately she started doing everything possible to improve her English. Soon she got a job as a head teller in one of the banks in Philadelphia. Today she and her family are happily living in the US. As members of the Ukrainian Baptist Church in Philadelphia, they are serving the Lord faithfully with the talents that He gave them.

Mykola served the Lord as a pastor of a church not far from Kiev, Ukraine. When he and his family had a chance to move to the United States, he was not sure that it was the will of God. He struggled with his feelings, but under the pressure of his family he agreed to move. People in the US welcomed them warmly. After a time of uncertainty about where God wanted them to live, they made a decision to move to a state where several Ukrainians were resettled. After 2 years of work as a bivocational pastor, he has a church of approximately 100 people. Today he and his family are certain that it was in God's plan for them to live and serve Him in the United States.

Cultural Characteristics

Family

For centuries, Ukrainians strongly believed that the foundation of a healthy society is a strong family. Most families had many children, and we were brought up under strict discipline. Because of economic situations, in most of the cases the family stayed together even when children were married and had their own children. Divorce, adultery, and fornication were considered shameful and disgraceful. Such sins were very rare.

However, in the last century, under the influence of other cultures and political systems, Ukrainians have changed a lot. Ukrainians living in foreign countries have adapted themselves to those cultures. For example, the ones in the former Soviet Union were devastated by the communist, atheistic government. Under such circumstances the family was weakened greatly.

Education

In the past, Ukrainians used to say, "School will not give you bread." With the coming of the Communist regime, Ukrainians were forced to go to school. Ten years of school (including high school) were mandatory. However, higher education was available just for those who were members of the Communist Party and atheists. Christians were not accepted in schools of higher learning. Most of the Ukrainians in the United States are blue-collar workers, but a good percentage are white-collar individuals.

Possessions

Ukrainians love to own things. For more than 70 years the Communist government worked hard to pull out this feeling from the hearts of the people. However, they did not succeed. Communism failed because it did not provide incentives for people to work hard. Ukrainians in the US are characterized as hard workers. Most belong to the middle class and some are considered rich.

Relationships

By nature, Ukrainians are friendly people. We like close relationships and usually are open to trust others and expect to be trusted. Even the long ordeal of Soviet domination did not destroy this wonderful tradition among Ukrainians. Many Ukrainians will not rush to have a close relationship. However, deep in their hearts, there is a thirst for close relationships. Ukrainians in the United States have adjusted themselves in some ways to the way of relationships of this country.

I believe the best method to win Ukrainians for the Lord is through a close and cordial friendship. After winning their confidence and friendship, their hearts are open to listen to and accept the gospel.

Inviting our non-Christian friends to have dinner with us in our homes is a very good occasion to witness to them about the grace of God. We value every expression of love and kindness. Still, even in those circumstances, it is important to be very sensitive and tactful. To go too fast and too far can ruin everything. In most cases, the conversion of Ukrainians is by way of evolution. Sometimes it takes years of close friendship and hard work to bring a Ukrainian to the Lord.

Approaches to Ministry and Witness

Ukrainians believe that the first person to bring the gospel to their land was the Apostle Andrew. Nevertheless, Ukraine (at that time, Kievan Rus) officially accepted Christianity as a state religion from Constantinople in A.D. 988. When the official Christian Church split in 1054, Ukraine automatically became a part of the eastern branch—the Orthodox Church. Later, some of the western provinces of Ukraine that were under the occupation of Poland accepted Catholicism. We can estimate the following: 50 percent of Ukrainians are Orthodox; 25 percent are Catholics; 10 percent are evangelicals; and 15 percent are pagans and atheists.

The evangelical movement in Ukraine is relatively new. The first born-again Christians were baptized in 1852. Many

believe that if we are Ukrainians, we have to be Orthodox
or Catholic. Evangelical churches are considered by many as
a foreign belief. At the beginning, evangelicals were brutally
persecuted by the official Church and the government.
During the Communist era, all Christians were persecuted.
Overall, evangelicals were always persecuted.

It is very hard for the Orthodox and the Catholics to
come and worship in evangelical churches. Ukrainians are
proud of their religions. Ukrainians in the US are well organized and work hard to preserve their culture, language,
and religion.

The most effective way to win Ukrainians for the Lord is
by a process of developing friendship and winning their
confidence. As was said, Ukrainians enjoy friendship.
Friendship is an open door to witness to them about what
we find in Jesus.

Evangelical services in an evangelical church building, in
most cases, will not be successful in attracting Ukrainians. It
is more advantageous to find a neutral ground, such as a
theater or educational center. In most large communities
where Ukrainians live, we have our own cultural centers
called *domkiva*. In such places we feel at home even with
an evangelical program. However, if you want Ukrainians to
attend such meetings, the program will have to include
cultural, traditional, and artistic selections.

The best way to motivate Ukrainians to attend services is
to have such meetings in conjunction with some special
event in the religious or national life of Ukraine, such as
Christmas, Easter, Shevchenko's Day, Independence Day,
and others.

Ukrainians respond very well to helping in different
projects when we are invited to participate. One of the
favorite ways for Ukrainians to participate in such events is
by singing in the choir or playing instruments in the orchestra.
Evangelistic services could require one united choir or separate choirs from different churches. Feeling a part of the
task, we will be involved in all aspects of the work.

As was mentioned before, most Ukrainians come to know Christ as their Savior through a long evangelistic process, rather than just by attending one evangelistic service. Still, such evangelistic services can be the culmination of a long process of work of the Holy Spirit. In most cases, Ukrainians will go to a pastor or deacon to say that they want to accept Jesus as their Savior. Many Ukrainians prefer to make their decision in an evolutionary way and so minimize the reaction from their environment. Therefore, it is very important to have trained believers to counsel and support new Ukrainian believers.

Another effective way to win Ukrainians for the Lord is through social ministries. Most new immigrants need all kinds of help. This is an open door to assist them in their material and physical needs and then satisfy their biggest need—the salvation of their souls.

Often when Ukrainians make their decision for Christ, they are already very well grounded in the teachings of the Bible and are ready to be baptized. Still, new converts need to be taught how to live a life of close relationship with the Lord and learn how to be good witnesses for Him.

John Kovalchuk
Philadelphia, Pennsylvania

GUIDELINES FOR LEADING
A GROUP STUDY

Gary Furr

- Read through the entire book first.
- Next, reread chapter 1 with your memory fresh from reading the ensuing chapters.
- With your Bible, notebook, and pencil at hand, read through the eight comments to follow. Make notes about who and what may be needed to create a setting conducive to healthy discussion and learning in this area.

As you call to mind the people who may be a part of your study group, make notes about questions you think you should raise for discussion. Ideally, you will have a working knowledge of the cultural mix in your neighborhood. Consider the opportunities you may have to initiate discussion about cultural issues in your locality.

Ideas to keep in mind
when planning the session
People can be quite defensive about their own way of life and culture. It is important that you allow people in the group to participate or sit back and observe if they so choose. Do not force participation. It is better to begin with common, universal, and nonthreatening experiences that can build cohesion before dealing with differences. Once, in a community where I was a pastor, I led a luncheon group where we came together to strengthen

relationships between various groups in our community. In our first meeting, I asked people in "forced" mixed small groups (i.e., in this case they were given numbered name tags so that they would not choose their regular group to sit with!), to talk about where they went to school when they were nine years old, who the disciplinarian was in their family, and so on. It was amazing to listen to the buzz of conversation!

We always begin with the assumption that there are God-given, universal, human similarities which can provide a basis for conversation. There are things ALL people do. Start there. But in an intensive workshop, you do want to get to the point.

FIRST, the leader must be very careful with words and attitudes. We may inadvertently betray our own cultural limitations (and probably will!).

SECOND, *relax!!* Sometimes I have found that laughter is one of the most powerful God-given antidotes to the self-seriousness of cultural differences. But be aware that humor is also culturally based. Sometimes, what is funny to one group only receives quizzical looks from others. Colloquial humor may not work unless you are careful to explain the cultural understanding underneath the particular practice or behavior you describe. For example, I led a retreat once for a group which included Sri Lankan students and immigrants. When I talked about issues of love and marriage, I discovered that in Sri Lanka, marriages are arranged by the family. So stories and issues about "selecting a mate" were irrelevant to some in my audience, unless I took the time to deal with that.

THIRD, in approaching the Bible study materials, I have purposely chosen stories rather than epistles or commandments. Stories provide a broad range of approaches for participants to enter in. Use the images and pictures in these stories for reflection. Jonah in the "whale," for example, is a wonderful image for reflection

on our motives, our relationship with God, opening up
to the possibility that we might need to change. The
same is true for Moab and Chemosh in the Ruth story.
How do we tell what is of Moab and what is neutral as
we approach another culture, for example? Missionaries
struggle with this all the time. Again, the same truth applies to the story of the woman at the well. Remember
that in addition to different cultures, you also have different kinds of personalities and temperaments present.
Some participants prefer lists that they can copy down
in lecture style. Others like picture images. Provide a variety of approaches so that the different ways of appre-
hending and experiencing are allowed expression.

FOURTH, when people come to a meeting that has as
its stated purpose "cross-cultural" anything, they come
with a great deal of anxiety as well as good will. A
warm, outgoing personality at the door to welcome
them to the session makes a great deal of difference.
Also, consider carefully the times when you undertake
lecture (not at 3:00 P.M., for example!).

FIFTH, I always assume that indirect is better than
broadside! Participation is what you want from the
group, not total agreement. Understanding and community building is, after all, the work of the Holy Spirit, not
simply the result of clever manipulation. So in addition
to structured times and events, *be sure there is time
enough for unstructured interaction* and further reflection. Pray for the meeting, provide for plenty of time
and space for interaction to occur.
Then trust God for the results.

The longer I lead meetings, the more I believe in
lengthy break times. *The break time is often when business
gets finished or a point can be picked up and continued by
two participants.* Be sure that you have a place, time, and
adequate provision for refreshments.

SIXTH, when I am working through Bible study
material such as this in a lecture fashion, I always try to
place a one page outline in the hands of the listeners, so
they will not have to work quite so hard to comprehend
where I am going. To those who are goal-oriented, the
knowledge of where the end of this presentation will be
is very reassuring.

SEVENTH, be certain that for discussion times you have
a facilitator who is capable of rephrasing, softening, finding the positive, and making connections between ideas.
This person also needs to be comfortable in the role,
nondefensive, and accepting to all. Sometimes, almost
inevitably in fact, there will be some in a group who
hold harsh or abrupt views or who are negative toward
the process. When they make statements that potentially
can disrupt, the facilitator needs to find ways to synthe-
size those comments into the group purpose or be able
to respond without being defensive. Not everyone can
do this well.

FINALLY, do your best to find a quiet, flexible setting
for the study. You will need space that lends itself to
both large-group discussion and small-group reflection.

Adapt the study to suit the needs of the group.

Following are some aspects of the four stories that you
might find helpful as beginning places in your preparation
for discussion. Be sure to have available Bibles and writing
materials for participants who may need them.
ALL OF THE RELATED SCRIPTURE TEXT SHOULD BE
READ BEFORE EACH DISCUSSION PHASE IS OPENED.

Ruth and Naomi
1. The nature of friendship.
2. How crisis is an opportunity for bonding.
3. Characteristics of open minds and hearts.
4. What is culture? Why are cultures different?

5. How do we tell the difference between essentials and non-essentials; i.e., what is cultural or what is universally true?

Jonah

1. Sympathize with Jonah. Why is it, for example, that we might run away from something God asks us to face? Why do people resist?
2. Help the group to think about the real human fears of others and where those come from.

Jesus and the Woman at the Well

1. You might approach the topic of unquestioned assumptions. What are they? It might be really revealing (even funny) for a group discussion of the things that various culture groups assume to be true without always knowing why. It also may be educational for others to discover that the things they always *thought* others believed are not necessarily so!
2. It is important for us to talk about how intentional we are about friendships with others. It is possible for us to pass our entire lives without moving out of our usual circles unless forced to do so. If Jesus is our model, what does it mean for us to think about "needing to go through Samaria"?

Philip and the Ethiopian Eunuch

1. Who are the people that we write off because they are not easy to reach? How did we make that decision?
2. It might be interesting to discuss or evaluate the unconscious curriculum in local churches, the unspoken assumptions that determine so many of our decisions like whom we will try to reach and whom we will not. Intention, the Spirit's leadership, and the ability to overcome the obstacles are all important parts of this process.
3. Delos Miles's book *Evangelizing the Hard to Reach* is an excellent resource. He has four categories that are very

helpful for thinking about our intentionality in reaching out to others.

Planning Session Review

1. Leader, be careful of your own words and attitudes.
2. Relax! Allow the healing antidotes of laughter and good humor to work for you.
3. Remember that stories provide a broad range of possibilities for participants to enter the discussion.
4. Allay the built-in anxiety of a cross-cultural dialogue by having warm, outgoing individuals to serve as greeters and hosts/hostesses.
5. Allow time for unstructured interaction among participants.
6. Provide a simple outline for participants to follow.
7. Provide a sensitive, yet capable facilitator who can enhance the flow of ideas and reflections.
8. Do your best to locate a quiet, adjustable setting for the study.

- From the time you learn that you will lead or be responsible for this study in a particular location, try to find out who is likely to attend. Learn as much about them in general terms as you can. Learn about the area, the cultural mix, the issues affecting the community, a little historical background on the community. The advantage for you is being able to indicate your concern about what affects participants in their day-to-day lives. More than anything else, this will open some channels for communication, however small. It may also help you understand the perspective they bring to the session and the context from which they respond.
- At the meeting, let your research be a secondary source of information. Find ways during the discussion to allow participants to tell their stories in their way. Their interest and input is part of their journey of involvement.
- Begin the study session in prayer, but be flexible about the closure. Let the dynamic of the group encounter

261.8348
C 619

LINCOLN CHRISTIAN COLLEGE AND SEMINARY

determine your closure. If the group seeks a follow-up session, consider the options for such a gathering. Determine the exact need, and plan accordingly. If other professional skills are needed, work with church staff and others to plan for such assistance.

- If your session concludes with a call for action with a particular culture group in mind, make plans immediately for another gathering to concentrate on specific steps toward that ministry goal. The needs are current and great. Don't lose a moment that you can invest in others for the glory of God!

3 4711 00151 8390